I0110867

Where is your Holy Spirit?

by D. Michael Cotten

©2018, D. Michael Cotten
All Rights Reserved

ISBN: 978-1-936497-37-9

Contact the Author at
dmichaelcotten@att.net

Searchlight Press
Who are you looking for?
Publishers of thoughtful Christian books since 1994.
PO Box 554
Henderson, TX 75653-0554
214.662.5494
info@Searchlight-Press.com
www.Searchlight-Press.com

Premise

GOD's act of Creation is finished, Jesus Christ's sacrifice for sin is finished, and Believers are living in the age of the Holy Spirit. The Church is more concerned with those in need of salvation than Believers in need of understanding the Holy Spirit and the benefits of salvation. Believers must develop a relationship with the Holy Spirit to fulfill the Lord's gift to Believers and bring glory to the Lord. A Believers purpose is reflecting to Heaven the image of God that they know and believe. The operative words are "**the GOD they know and believe**". The reality of the God in the Believers life is measured by their knowledge of GOD and experience with the Holy Spirit, measured as barely acquainted to intimate Friend.

A Believer's Spiritual vocation is to steward the assets of GOD's Creation for the benefit of others. Just as God started the world into motion and then rested, and Jesus sacrificed himself and said, "it is finished", GOD sent the Holy Spirit to Believers to act in all the areas of grace. Now, in this present time, Jesus Christ has sent Himself in Spirit form to abide with Believers, to show us all the gifts of grace given to Believers; salvation, justification, deliverance, healing, prosperity, and everything needed for the abundant life and Godliness. GOD gave the earth to Mankind and gave Believers authority to steward the earth.

The positive performance of Christian Believers toward others, is the action that can reflect the image of God back to Heaven and bring glory to our Savior and the Holy Spirit. Jesus said, "He came to serve, not to be served." Think about this: **If accumulating wealth was important to GOD**, Believers would be able to keep your wealth when you die. A Believer is God's delivery system to the world. God gave you the power to build wealth. The daily decisions for Believers is to act, GOD-centered and steward God's blessings for the benefit of others or self-centered convinced that your ability will supply your needs through your own power?

Failure to steward GOD's creation for the benefit of others is dangerous to Believers and to GOD's creation because it relinquishes a Believers power and authority to the forces that tear down the fabric of the World, namely the devil and his evil influence. Our lives and the fabric of the world is dependent on the authority used by Believers from, "**the GOD we know and believe** ". Believers are the arms and legs God has to deliver the grace given to Believers for others. The problem to be considered is the Believers influence and authority is to be used for the benefit of others and not all consumed on ourselves. Do you, as a Believer, understand the new covenant of Eternal life is sealed with the Holy Spirit for action? **GOD is inside you, the root of perfect love is inside you!** The new creation life is a dynamic and powerful force for good, but a Believer can keep the force in a private place by believing that a ticket to Heaven is what you received from Jesus Christ's sacrifice and your new Creation life starts after you die. You may go to Heaven, but live a dull life without ever entering the Kingdom of GOD, but there is a better way.

Churches concentrate on introducing seekers to Jesus in two hours a week, and do not have enough of each Believer's time to adequately teach everything you need to know about God, the Son, and the Holy Spirit. It is the personal responsibility of the Believer to learn about GOD and the Post-cross life and its benefits. This book will focus on living GOD-centered and not self-centered lives, reflecting the image of your creator back to Heaven. The Golden Rule and stewarding of GOD's creation is our good service. Happiness and prosperity comes with service just like the reward of the productive stewards in the parable of the talents. Matthew 25:14

GOD-centered

When a Believer is GOD-centered every part of your life is in order. Every promise and prophecy that Father GOD and Jesus Christ created by their words and deeds were given to Believers and the Holy Spirit is given to guide the Believers into all the gifts of GOD. The blessings given to Believers are listed in Deuteronomy 28, the 91st Psalm, Isaiah 53, and the 103rd Psalm and many more. In addition, Jesus has taken away the curse of the law. Believers are powerful and have a mission to listen to GOD and fulfill GOD's will by being in a certain place at a certain time to fulfill an act that GOD has planned, to answer the prayer of someone in need. Believers are the hands and legs GOD uses to fulfill His will and acts of kindness and supply on Earth.

Self-centered persons are subject to missing salvation altogether and Believers can seriously limit the power of a life with the Holy Spirit by focusing on their life without regard to others and without the gift of the Holy Spirit.

Listen to the Lord when He spoke about being double minded:

> Revelation 3:15 "'I know your works: you are neither cold nor hot. Would that you were either cold or hot! So, because you are lukewarm, and neither hot nor cold, I will spit you out of my mouth. For you say, I am rich, I have prospered, and I need nothing, not realizing that you are wretched, pitiable, poor, blind, and naked.

Words from the Author

Writing Style

This book is not written in strict adherence to grammatical rules. The Bible and concepts of GOD are complicated. To unpack the compound sentences and the interaction of the visible and invisible world; each page will contain highlights, capital letters, quotes, underlines and cascading verses, to add sound and definition to the words.

Table of Contents

Foundational information
for understanding the Bible and
the Post-cross life with the Holy Spirit.

The following concepts and scriptures are necessary to understand the Post- Cross life given to Believers and to understand how to study the New Testament.

<u>Pre-requisites</u> for a Holy Spirit "thrilled" life in the Post-Cross world;

> **Belief that GOD created the worlds** and the system for the reproduction of every living organism, control of all the elements and forces in the visible, and the invisible worlds.

> **Belief in Jesus Christ as Savior** of the World and the redeemer of all sin for the Believer: *past, present, and future.*

> **Belief and understanding of the gift of the Holy Spirit** to seal Believers Eternal life by abiding inside Believers in our inner sanctum. The Holy Spirit teaches Believers about the deep things of GOD and offers Believers joint operations with the power of the Spiritual world.

<u>Understanding God's presence in the Post-Cross world;</u>

> **Father GOD** is in Heaven, on the Throne, in the Heaven's Temple, a Temple not made with hands.

> **Our Brother, Jesus Christ,** is at the right hand of Father GOD.

> **Our Best Friend, the Holy Spirit,** is inside Believers in a Temple not made by hands but made by GOD. 2nd Corinthians 5:1

<u>Understanding the plurality of our GOD and the Trinity's accomplishments;</u>

> **Father GOD** created the world and the reproduction systems for the automatic continuation of all life and control of the

atomic elemental world until GOD's next creation, "The New Jerusalem".

Jesus Christ paid the sin debt "once and for all" for Believer's" past, present, and in the future.

The Holy Spirit is the power that raised Jesus Christ from the dead and that same power is now abiding with and inside Believers baptized in the Holy Spirit.

Understanding the timing and significance of each age of the world and GOD.

Father GOD created the world and said, "It is good" and created Mankind and said, "It is very good" and **GOD has not created anything pertaining to the continuation of the world since.**

Jesus Christ paid the sin debt and fulfilled all the promises in The Old Testament pertaining to "the Promise", sin, and the curse. Jesus gave "his finished works" to Believers as an inheritance. **Jesus Christ is not coming down from Heaven to die on the cross again.** Paying the debt is finished. The inheritance is yours, the Believer must use the inheritance, or it just sits in the Believer's account doing nothing, bringing no Glory to our Lord, The Father, nor benefit to the Believer. **The Holy Spirit** has been given to all Believers and a relationship is available to any Believer who asks. The power transfer from Jesus being "with" mankind in human form to being "inside Believers", in the person of the Holy Spirit is super natural. Jesus, with us, is now GOD inside us.

Understanding GOD's Plan
Old Covenant - New Covenant
Before the Cross – After the Cross

The New Covenant does not start at Mathew 1:1, the New Covenant does not start at Jesus birth, the New Covenant does not begin until Jesus takes the sins of the entire world and offers forgiveness to all Believers. When studying the Word of GOD, Believers must rightly divide the Word of GOD. Salvation through Jesus Christ cannot begin until Jesus goes to the Cross (Post-Cross). One of the keys to understanding GOD's Word is to examine which covenant the scripture references. Your red-letter edition of your Bible is important, but the words Jesus spoke must be rightly divided into the context that applied to Old Covenant and/or the New Covenant. Jesus lived during the era of the old Covenant. The requirements for Believers' actions **before the Cross and after the Cross** are completely different. The difference in the context of each covenant may cause Believers to fall victim to a performance based Christianity that is far below the level of life Jesus died to give Believers.

For example; Salvation

New Testament instructions for the Old Covenant (**Pre-Cross way to Salvation**)

Listen to Jesus regarding Salvation to the rich young ruler;

> And a certain ruler asked him, saying, Good Master, what shall **I do to inherit eternal life?** And Jesus said unto him, why callest thou me good? none is good, save one, that is, God. <u>Thou knowest the commandments, Do not commit adultery, Do not kill, Do not steal, Do not bear false witness, Honour thy father and thy mother</u>. And he (the young ruler) said, All these have I kept from my youth up. Now when Jesus heard these things, he said unto him, Yet lackest thou one thing: sell all that thou hast, and distribute unto the poor, and thou shalt have treasure in heaven: and come, follow me. Luke 18

Before the Lord's Sacrifice for Sin, "the way" to Salvation was "Do the Commandments and follow Jesus". (**Pre-cross**)

Now listen to the change after the Cross; (**Post-cross way to Salvation**) Apostle Paul in Acts talking to the Jailer about Salvation;

> And at midnight Paul and Silas prayed, and sang praises unto God: and the prisoners heard them. And suddenly there was a great earthquake, so that the foundations of the prison were shaken: and immediately all the doors were opened, and every one's bands were loosed. And the keeper of the prison awaking out of his sleep, and seeing the prison doors open, he drew out his sword, and would have killed himself, supposing that the prisoners had been fled. But Paul cried with a loud voice, saying, do thyself no harm: for we are all here. Then he called for a light, and sprang in, and came trembling, and fell down before Paul and Silas, and brought them out, and said, Sirs, what must I do to be saved? **And they said, believe on the Lord Jesus Christ, and thou shalt be saved, and thy house.** Acts 16

This miracle of Salvation was not available when Christ was teaching on Earth, but available to Believers after Jesus went to the Cross. The scripture above confirms in context, showing the difference between Pre-cross and Post-cross Salvation (**Post-cross**).

Another **Post-cross** Salvation confirmation; The Apostle John confirms Belief in Jesus Christ, without any required performance, is the way to eternal life and the context is the New Covenant.

> **For God so loved the world,** that he gave his only begotten Son, that **whosoever believeth in him should not perish, but have everlasting life.** For God sent not his Son into the world to condemn the world; but that the world through him might be saved. John 3:16-17

This scripture is Post-cross because you cannot believe in Jesus Christ for Eternal life until Jesus had gone to the Cross.

Another Illustration of the difference between **Pre-cross and Post-cross covenant concerns forgiveness from GOD**;

GOD required performance in the **Pre-cross covenant**; Believers must forgive others to get forgiven by GOD.

> The next three scriptures reveal a requirement or performance required before blessing from GOD in the Pre-cross era.

>> And forgive us our debts, as we forgive our debtors. **Matthew 6:12**

>> For if ye forgive men their trespasses, your heavenly Father will also forgive you: **Matthew 6:14**

>> But if ye forgive not men their trespasses, neither will your Father forgive your trespasses. **Matthew 6:15**

In the Pre-cross Covenant, a Believer had to forgive "first" to have GOD forgive them, later.

In the Post-Cross Covenant;

Teachings on forgiveness after the beginning of the New Covenant (post-cross), the Apostle Paul tells Believers that Believers have been forgiven for all sins by Christ Jesus and therefore Believers should forgive others.

> And be ye kind one to another, tenderhearted, forgiving one another, **even as God for Christ's sake hath forgiven you.** Ephesians 4:32

> Beloved, if God so loved us, we ought also to love one another.

> I John 4:11

Forgiveness is no longer performance based, a Believer's forgiveness **came at the Cross.** Living without condemnation is important to the Human experience. Acknowledging the Lord's forgiveness toward us, so that we can forgive ourselves and stay in the Lord's Peace is very important. Jesus did away with the universe of sin, now Believers can forgive hurts from others because we have been forgiven and loved by GOD. Now that I know I am forgiven of every sin; when I do something, I am not proud of doing, I still apologize to Lord Jesus acknowledging His sacrifice and love for me, but not asking Jesus to come die again as if His sacrifice did not cover this new transgression. There is no condemnation for those in Christ Jesus.

Jesus was our Savior 2,000 years ago. Jesus is our High Priest now, and today Believers are connected to Jesus by the Holy Spirit, who is abiding in Believers. Again, think about the construction of the New Testament: Jesus was with Mankind on Earth during the Synoptic Gospels and Acts and GOD is inside Believers after his ascension to Heaven in Acts. Everything that Jesus accomplished for Believers through Salvation was done two thousand years ago and must be appropriated by your faith in the gift and promise of the Holy Spirit inside Believers by Jesus Christ.

At the Cross: The Lord's blood redeemed the Believers sin, His stripes healed our diseases, on His shoulders He bore our sorrows and carried our griefs, He was pierced for our transgressions, His body was bruised for our iniquities, He was punished to bring us peace, and He was made poor that we might become rich. All of the finished works of Jesus Christ were accomplished and are all part of the Believers Post-cross inheritance. A Believers inheritance from the Cross and the indwelling of the Holy Spirit is the power of the New Creation life and must be believed and acted on by faith, and Jesus gave to every Believer "the Measure of faith". Romans 12:3

GOD writes the New Covenant
in a Believers Mind and heart.

Think about the change in wording used **pre-cross and post-cross** in relationship to Jesus and his disciples. **Disciple** is a person training under the discipline or teaching of another. The word disciple is used in the four Gospels 200 times and in Acts 35 times and not once after the ascension of Jesus to Heaven. There has been a change, **After the Cross** the teacher is inside the Believer. Do not miss the importance of the change in the Post-cross new testament from Disciple to "In Christ". Believers are no longer disciples of Jesus teachings GOD has written his words in our hearts and Jesus is sending His Spirit to indwell Believers to bring revelation.

GOD announces that Believers will be taught by the Holy Spirit and the Word of GOD.

> Hebrews 8:10 For this is the covenant that I will make with the house of Israel after those days (**post-cross**), declares the Lord: **I will put my laws (instructions) into their minds, and write them on their hearts, and I will be their God, and they shall be my people.**

Listen to these four examples of Pre-cross and Post-cross doctrines that are important to understanding GOD's grace;

> The way to salvation is by grace not works.
>
> Forgive others because Believers have been forgiven.
>
> Believers are now a member of God's family. Jesus is our Brother, and the Holy Spirit is our friend.
>
> GOD has written His New Covenant on a Believers heart by infilling Believers with the Holy Spirit.

After the Cross, the Apostles Paul and John teach Believers about a personal, active, intimate, relationship with Jesus Christ through the Holy Spirit. The only way a Believer can have a relationship with Jesus after His cross experience is through the Holy Spirit. There is a change in the New Testament Personification of Jesus to the Holy

Spirit; notice the new terms "In Him", "In whom", "In Christ", and "in the Spirit".

Notice the new description of our relationship with Jesus **after the Cross is different. Think about the words used after the Cross. The word disciple is not used again and that relationship with Christ is replaced with; In Christ, in Him, in whom, in the Spirit, and Brother.**

> **In Him** meaning with GOD inside Believers and Believers inside GOD, "In Him" is used 70 times in the New Testament with 66 times **after** the Synoptic Gospels concentrated in John and Paul's writings. **In Christ** is the New covenant word for Disciples. "In Christ" is used 78 times after the ascension and not one time in the Gospels, because Jesus had not died and been resurrected. Believers can't be **in Him** until Jesus had been resurrected.
>
> When a believer is acting in his authority or using the Name of Jesus, they are **in the Spirit.** Believers could not use the "Name of Jesus" until **after the Cross.**

Another illustration of a **post-cross change** is the Believers familial relationship with GOD; Jesus calls his followers, "Brothers" after the resurrection and announces that GOD is Father to all Believers.

> (John 20:17) Jesus tells Mary; "Go tell **my brothers** I am about to ascend to my Father and **your Father**".

At His Resurrection, Believers were added to the **Family of GOD.** Before the Lord's resurrection, **Jesus had never** referred to the disciples and entourage as **brothers.** Do not miss this, if Jesus is your brother you are part of GOD's family.

Pre-Cross and Post-Cross prayer has changed.

Pre-cross; Jesus gave disciples the model prayer.

Matthew 6:9 Pray then like this: "Our Father in heaven, hallowed be your name. Your kingdom come, your will be done, on earth as it is in heaven. Give us this day our daily bread, and forgive us our debts, as we forgive our debtors. And lead us not into temptation, but deliver us from evil.

This prayer was pre-cross and before GOD's will was done on earth as it is in Heaven and Jesus restored righteousness in the Earth. This prayer contains the words of Jesus and was perfect in its time, but Jesus has changed the world with His death, resurrection, and sending of the Holy Spirit. As the Lord's sacrifice was approaching Jesus gave this comforting word:

As Jesus was preparing the disciples for his leaving, His teachings for a post-cross world was, "Speak to this mountain and it should obey you." And "Greater works than I have done shall you do because I go to the Father." and GOD sent Believers the Holy Spirit. Is your Church teaching you with hymns and prayers to try to move GOD for your benefit? God can't be moved; GOD is the same yesterday, today, and forever and Creator God and Jesus have proclaimed they are finished and the new era is full of power through the Holy Spirit inside Believers. Believers are now Stewards of GOD's world full of the Holy Spirit and power for the benefit of others.

The post-cross prayer, went to a higher level when forgiven Believers, full of the Holy Spirit, are given the authority to pray in the Name of Jesus.

Mark 16:15 And he said unto them, Go ye into all the world, and preach the gospel to every creature. He that believeth and is baptized shall be saved; but he that believeth not shall be damned. And these signs shall follow them that believe; In my name shall they cast out devils; they shall speak with new tongues; They shall take up serpents; and if they drink any deadly thing, it shall not hurt them; they shall lay hands on the sick, and they shall recover.

This is a pre-cross scripture but is not about a post-cross subject. Note; Not once did Jesus send demons and afflictions on people, but instead Jesus said, "In my name" cast out devils, heal the sick, and more.

Now listen to Paul describe the Believers blessed with the Holy Spirit, a new Father, and the Name of Jesus; listen to these five scriptures;

John proclaimed: Acts 10:38 how God anointed Jesus of Nazareth with **the Holy Spirit** and **with power.** He went about doing good and healing all who were oppressed by the devil, for God was **with him**.

"Brothers, what shall we do?" Act 2:38 And Peter said to them, "Repent and be baptized every one of you **in the name of Jesus Christ** for the forgiveness of your sins, and you will receive the gift of the Holy Spirit.

Ephesians 5:18 And do not get drunk with wine, for that is debauchery, but be filled with the Spirit, addressing one another in psalms and hymns and spiritual songs, singing and making melody to the Lord with your heart, giving thanks always and for everything to God the Father **in the name of our Lord Jesus Christ**

Colossians 3:16 And be thankful. Let the word of Christ dwell in you richly, teaching and admonishing one another in all wisdom, singing psalms and hymns and spiritual songs, with thankfulness in your hearts to God. And whatever you do, in word or deed, do everything **in the name of the Lord**

Jesus, giving thanks to God the Father through him.

2nd Thessalonians 1:11 To this end we always pray for you, that our God may make you worthy of his calling and may fulfill every resolve for good and every work of faith by his power, so that **the name of our Lord Jesus** may be glorified in you, and you in him, according to the grace of our God and the Lord Jesus Christ.

After the Cross when speaking, praying, and acting **in the Name of Jesus,** there is power to act and a play book for living in power.

Before the Cross
Gentiles were not even a people.
After the Cross we are GOD's family.

Listen to the Apostle Paul describe the Believers adoption into GOD's Chosen people and into God's family. Listen to this proof from Ephesians;

Christ is the reason we are now at peace. He made us Jews **and you who are not Jews** one people. We were separated by a wall of hate that stood between us, but Christ broke down that wall. By giving his own body, **Christ ended the law with its many commands and rules.** His purpose was to make the two groups become **one in him.** By doing this he would make peace. Through the cross Christ ended the hate between the two groups. And after they became one body, he wanted to bring them both back to God. **He did this with his death on the cross.** Christ came and brought the message of peace to you non-Jews who were far away from God. And he brought that message of peace to those who were near to God.

Yes, through Christ we all have the right to come to the Father in one Spirit. So now you non-Jewish people are not visitors or strangers, but you are citizens together with God's holy people. **You belong to God's family.** You Believers are like a building that God owns. That building was built on the foundation that the apostles and prophets prepared. Christ Jesus himself is the most important stone in that building. The whole building is joined together in Christ, and he makes it grow and become a holy temple in the Lord. Ephesians 2:12-2

Note; Worship is love expressed.

Communion is a Post-Cross Weapon
Given to Believers

Before Jesus went to the Cross (Pre-cross) there were laws concerning meat and drink and Holy days, Post-Cross, the Lord, has given Believers three acknowledgments to the Spiritual world; Baptism in water, Baptism with the Holy Spirit, and Communion. Each acknowledgment is an entry into the Spiritual world and is an act of worship. Think about it, each external sign or acknowledgment is a visible sign for a Spiritual experience.

Communion is more than a once a week or once a month ritual at Church. **It is more than** an Institution of the Church, it is for all Believers when led by your Spirit. It is the basis for being GOD-Centered and should be done often. Communion teaches Believers to look into the Spiritual world, everything that the Lord has for Believers comes from the Spiritual world. Listen to the Scripture;

Matthew 26:26 And as they were eating, Jesus took bread, and blessed *it,* and brake *it,* and gave *it* to the disciples, and said, Take, eat; this is my body. And he took the cup, and gave thanks, and gave *it* to them, saying, Drink ye all of it; For this is my blood of the new testament, which is shed for many for the remission of sins.

Jesus said, "This do in remembrance of me." Believers must look with the eyes of your Spirit to imagine the bread as Christ's body and the cup as the Lord's blood. The horrendous death on the Cross was the price Jesus paid for your and my right standing with GOD Almighty. The Post-Cross world is Spiritual and Believers must practice looking into the Spiritual world. **Stop, think about it,** practice looking into the Spirit world and seeing the Lord's body crushed for you and meditate on what it means to you. What does the Lord's blood mean to you? The Lord said, "This do in remembrance of me" and not once a month at church, but take communion as often as you need to keep Believers in remembrance of a living GOD.

The most important event since "Creation" was the resurrection of Jesus Christ, and it was vital that the Lord's chosen apostles witnessed the resurrection. The most important event since resurrection of Jesus Christ is the giving of the Holy Spirit to abide with believers and to teach them about the gifts God has for those who believe.

Acknowledge and Worship

It is important to understand the significance of the three roles of GOD: GOD in the creation, redemption and abiding in Believers.

It is important to understand Creation of the world and to know that everything in the world was set in motion by GOD 6,000 plus years ago and will continue until God acts.

It is important to understand that Salvation was set in motion nearly 2,000 years ago. Salvation is appropriated through belief in your need for a savior and in Jesus Christ and his atonement for sin. Can you believe that something that happened two thousand years ago can be relevant today?

It is important for Believers to know; the new Covenant does not start at Matthew 1:1. It starts when Jesus sends Believers the Holy Spirit and power at Pentecost. The new Covenant is a post-cross event and Jesus, who had a human body, handed His Earthly ministry, over to the Holy Spirit.

Jesus sent Believers, the Holy Spirit, the same Holy Spirit, that GOD, the Father, sent to be on Jesus, at His baptism. At the Cross there was **just one righteous Man** and after the Cross, with the gift of the Holy Spirit, billions of Believers are made righteous. What are Believers to do with this fact? Do you know the Holy Spirit, that is inside you, and if not why and what are you doing in conjunction with the Holy Spirit?

Do not wait on the Church to take Communion, Communion is the remembrance of the finished works of Jesus Christ given to Believers, that brings the confidence to act in faith, to reign in life, and Steward GOD's world for the benefit of others.

GOD's plan

The era of the Holy Spirit was and is meant to be greater than the era of Jesus Christ because Jesus has joined the Father in Heaven and sent the Holy Spirit with eternal life for Believers.

This book will try to rightly divide GOD's word and highlight the abundant life that GOD has given Believers through the Holy Spirit and offer motivation to Believers to have a more intimate relationship with GOD through His Spirit inside you.

Notes

We can only come to GOD through Jesus Christ
We can only come to Jesus through the Holy Spirit.

Chapter One

Startling Fact:
Jesus needed the Holy Spirit
and Believers in Jesus do also.

Jesus did not start His ministry and the mighty miracles until the Holy Spirit came on and stayed on Jesus at His Baptism. Jesus was near thirty years old as He started his ministry. There is not one recorded miracle before the Holy Spirit of God Almighty was sent to be on and in Jesus Christ at His baptism. The Spiritual world for Believers must also combine Salvation of Jesus Christ and the abiding of the Holy Spirit. The "Post Cross" life for Believers is new and powerful because The Holy Spirit is inside and staying on Believers. The same Holy Spirit that was on Jesus and raised Him from the dead is available to Believers. It is the addition of the Holy Spirit to the Believers life that allows the Believer **to rest from your works** and join with the Holy Spirit to do the works GOD had planned for Believers.

The only man on earth, other than Jesus, blessed with the Holy Spirit before the Holy Spirit was given to Believers was John the Baptist. Listen to Jesus compare John the Baptist to Believers;

> Luke 7:27 This is he of whom it is written, "'Behold, I send my messenger before your face, who will prepare your way before you.' I tell you, among those born of women none is greater than John (the Baptist). Yet the one who is least in the kingdom of God is greater than he."

Think about the Lord's words describing, John the Baptist, He was the greatest man that ever lived, but because John died, before Jesus went to the Cross, he was not blessed with salvation, while he was living, nor was he able to enter the Kingdom of GOD while he was living. The Salvation offered by Jesus Christ is post-cross and brings righteousness to Believers and that redemption makes the Believers greater than the John, the Baptist. John was not blessed with eternal life, while living, because John died before Jesus went to the cross.

The Believer's post-cross life starts with receiving the Holy Spirit.

Believers must understand the change in relationship with GOD from Jesus Christ to the Holy Spirit. Jesus has ascended to Heaven as Believers advocate with God and has sent Believers the Holy Spirit to power the New Creation life. **The transference of Jesus with a human body to the Holy Spirit of God Almighty is the most important era in History and you are living it, if you received the Holy Spirit after you believed.**

To receive the Holy Spirit, the Believer must ask for and believe the Lord wants to give you the Holy Spirit and you must believe that you have received the Holy Spirit inside you, because GOD's word says so. A Believer, to be successful must believe that the power in the new creation life is "Jesus and Father God have completed everything necessary for the promises of the Bible to be available" The promises of the Spirit must be seen or imagined as given to the Believer with the eye of faith in your heart. To operate in your faith a Believer must talk to and listen to the Holy Spirit to activate the promises stored up for the Believers. Consider the instructions of Jesus as he ascended to His Father and your Father. Jesus, preparing for the ascension into

Heaven, tells the Apostles **do not start** on the "New Creation Life" until you have received the Holy Spirit **and power.**

> Luke 24:49 And, behold, I send the promise of my Father (Holy Spirit) upon you: but tarry ye in the city of Jerusalem, until ye be endued with power from on high.

The Disciples were saved, GOD was "with" mankind in Jesus Christ (Human form) and now GOD, the Holy Spirit is abiding "inside" Believers in a Temple not made with hands (Spirit form).

First, Believers need to know you can be saved and not know about the Holy Spirit. Listen to Paul at Corinth talking to believers;

> Acts 19:1 … at Corinth, Paul passed through the inland country and came to Ephesus. There he found some disciples. And he said to them, **"Did you receive the Holy Spirit when you believed?"** And they said, **"No, we have not even heard that there is a Holy Spirit."**

> Acts 19:4 Then said Paul, John verily baptized with the baptism of repentance, saying unto the people, that they should believe on him which should come after him, that is, on Christ Jesus. When they heard *this,* **they were baptized in the name of the Lord Jesus.** And when Paul had laid *his* hands upon them, the Holy Spirit came on them; and they spake with tongues, and prophesied.

Don't be distracted by the speaking in tongues, not everyone speaks with tongues, or a prayer language the Believer does not understand, but you will miss the power of God inside you, if you do not ask for and embrace the gift of the Holy Spirit. Not only is the Holy Spirit available to live inside Believers but when the Believer is Born-again, God makes a special place inside you for the Holy Spirit and your new born-again Spirit to abide. If Jesus Christ insisted on the Disciples and friends to tarry in Jerusalem until they receive the Holy Spirit and power. Can new age Believers go without the Holy Spirit and all that receiving the Holy Spirit entails?

The Holy Spirit is just one of the finished works of Jesus given to Believers. The Finished works of Jesus like the Fruit of the Spirit is the Believer's possession, **you own it.** Asking for the finished works in prayer, is a prayer that Jesus cannot answer because Jesus is "finished". Believers own, salvation, redemption, redeemed from the curse, health, peace, prosperity, and more are fulfilled and given to believers at the Cross. Jesus is the fulfillment of Isiah 53 and Psalms 103 and these promises are now the inheritance of Believers and must be appropriated by Believers. When the Apostle Paul asked for the thorn in his side to be removed GOD said,

> "My grace is <u>sufficient </u>for you, for my power is made perfect in weakness." 2nd Corinthians 12:9

The question for Believers is "How to appropriate the grace of GOD and power of the Holy Spirit for victory in the abundant life?" Listen to Paul tell us what was his thorn in the flesh;

> And lest I should be exalted above measure through the abundance of the revelations, there was given to me a thorn in the flesh, **the messenger of Satan to buffet me,** lest I should be exalted above measure. 2nd Corinthians 12:7

The Holy Spirit is the grace of God to stand against the messengers of Satan.

Believers contain
The Temple of the Holy Spirit

It is exciting to know that Believers are the Temple of GOD. Listen to the Apostle Paul's description;

> 1st Corinthians 3:16 Know ye not that ye are the temple of God, and *that* the Spirit of God dwelleth in you?

Again, in Corinthians the Apostle Paul announces that Believers are the Temple of the living GOD.

> What agreement has the temple of God with idols? For we are the temple of the living God; as God said, **"I will make my dwelling among them and walk among them, and I will be their God, and they shall be my people.** Therefore go out from their midst, and be separate from them, says the Lord, and touch no unclean thing; **then I will welcome you, and I will be a father to you, and you shall be sons and daughters to me, says the Lord Almighty."** 2nd Corinthians 6:15

Take a minute or more to meditate on this scripture; a Believer is the Temple of GOD and God is abiding with you and God is now your Father and you are His child. There is more.

Now John, the Baptist, adds a new description to receiving the Baptism by Jesus Christ of the Holy Spirit, by adding "and fire".

> Luke 3:16   John answered, saying unto *them* all, I indeed baptize you with water; but one mightier than I cometh, the latchet of whose shoes I am not worthy to unloose: **he shall baptize you with the Holy Spirit and with fire:**

Is there a Biblical significance to being the Temple of GOD, and being baptized by Jesus Christ with **the Baptism of the Holy Spirit and fire? The answer is yes,** at the dedication of each Temple, the Lord, demonstrated the occasion with fire and Believers are now the Temple of GOD and fire should be part of the Believers Baptism and new Temple of the presence of GOD in each believer.

Fire from Heaven

How did fire play a role in the dedication of new Temples of God, in the Old Testament? Is there any connection to the New Testament and the Post-Cross era? The answer is yes, and it may surprise you. At the dedication to the Temple of Moses which moved with the tribes for the forty years in the desert. The following happened;

> Leviticus 9:22 Then Aaron lifted up his hands toward the people and blessed them, and he came down from offering the sin offering and the burnt offering and the peace offerings. And Moses and Aaron went into the tent of meeting, and when they came out they blessed the people, and the **glory of the LORD appeared to all the people.** And <u>fire came</u> out from before the LORD and consumed the burnt offering and the pieces of fat on the altar, and when all the people saw it, they shouted and fell on their faces.

At the dedication of the Second Temple, built by Solomon. This transpired;

> **2ⁿᵈ Chronicles 7:1** As soon as Solomon finished his prayer, **fire came** down from heaven and consumed the burnt offering and the sacrifices, and the glory of the LORD filled the temple. And the priests could not enter the house of the LORD, because **the glory of the LORD filled the LORD's house.** When all the people of Israel saw the **fire come down** and the **glory of the LORD** on the temple, they bowed down with their faces to the ground on the pavement and worshiped and gave thanks to the LORD, saying, "For he is good, for his steadfast love endures forever."

Later in the New Testament and in the Post-Cross era Luke describes the coming of the Holy Spirit like this;

> Acts 2:2 And suddenly there came from heaven a sound like a mighty rushing wind, and it filled the entire house where they were sitting. And divided tongues as of fire appeared to

them and rested on each one of them. And they were all filled with the Holy Spirit and began to speak in other tongues as the Spirit gave them utterance.

Each and every Believer must ask the Lord to be baptized with the Holy Spirit and with fire and must believe they have received the Holy Spirit because GOD promised, and GOD keeps his promises. **The Bible confirms that Believers contain the Temple of God and abiding in the Temple is the Holy Spirit and the Believers Born-again Spirit forever joined together in eternity.** Believers know that GOD has created the World and your body and Believers should use that fact to build your foundation for belief in the Spiritual world where GOD's Spirit lives. There is absolute proof of the life of Jesus Christ and that fact, should give Believers additional faith for believing in the Holy Spirit. The Holy Spirit is part of your inheritance from Jesus Christ. Jesus came and died to give Believers the righteousness necessary for the Holy Spirit to have a righteous place to abide inside Believers.

> John 6:28 Then said they unto him, What shall we do, that we might work the works of God? **Jesus answered and said unto them, This is the work of God, that ye believe on Jesus whom GOD hath sent.**

Believers must believe in Jesus to do the mighty works of GOD. These works are not the works to deserve the promises of Jesus Christ, but through belief in the GOD of Creation, Jesus Christ, and the Holy Spirit; Believers will do acts of kindness that glorify GOD.

In Remembrance of Me
Jesus Promises the Holy Spirit

The Holy Spirit is given to Believers for comfort and peace by Jesus Christ from God Almighty. Imagine!! part of GOD Almighty lives inside Believers. Let the Apostle John's description of this transference from Jesus in human form to the Holy Spirit, give you comfort;

> John 14:15 If ye love me, keep my commandments. And I will pray the Father, and **GOD shall give you another Comforter, that The Holy Spirit may abide with you forever;** Even the Spirit of truth; whom the world cannot receive, because it seeth him not, neither knoweth him: but ye know The Holy Spirit; for he dwelleth with you, and **shall be in you.** I will not leave you comfortless: **I will come to you.** Yet a little while, and the world seeth me no more; but ye see me: because I live, ye shall live also.

Notice; That Jesus is saying, after a Believer receives the Holy Spirit you will be able to know Jesus in the Spirit. Remember Jesus is the Truth and His Spirit will be in you.

Think about communion with the Lord, when you take the bread and the cup you are partaking of Jesus body and blood. If you will open your eyes to the Spirit, and discern with your heart the Lord Jesus body, you can see with your Spiritual eyes. Instead of imagining Jesus on the cross, imagine Jesus at the right hand of the Father speaking to GOD about you. You are his brother and part of God is inside Believers.

Jesus teaching about the Post-Cross life.

> "I have told you these things while I am still with you. But the Counselor, the Holy Spirit, whom the Father will send in my name, **will teach you everything; that is, he will remind you of everything I have said to you.** "What I am leaving with you is my peace. (sozo) Total wellbeing"— John 14

The importance of the preceding scriptures is Jesus revealing to Believers that the Holy Spirit is the **next part of GOD's plan for**

Believers. Peace and God's rest is the harvest of a relationship with Almighty GOD through the Holy Spirit. If Believers are open to the Spiritual world inside them, you are ready to reign in life. To further the understanding of the work of the Holy Spirit, think about the word "sozo" used by Jesus in John 14 to be peace. It is translated 57 times as saved, and 53 times as peace, healed, delivered, and made whole. Salvation is not just a ticket to Heaven but can be total wellbeing.

> **Meditate on the scriptures about the Lord's death;** The Lord's blood redeemed the Believers sin, by His stripes He has healed our diseases, on His shoulders He bore our sorrows and carried our griefs, He was pierced for our transgressions, His body was bruised for our iniquities, He was punished to bring us peace, and He was made poor that we might become rich. Isaiah 53. 2nd Corinthians 8:9

> **Messianic prophecy for Believers;** Who forgives all your iniquity, who heals all your diseases, who redeems your life from the pit, who crowns you with steadfast love and mercy, who satisfies you with good so that your youth is renewed like the eagle's. Psalms 103

If you believe in salvation by Jesus Christ. What can keep you from believing in the Holy Spirit and the finished works of Jesus Christ, your Savior?

Listen to the words of Jesus about the peace available to Believers, the following scripture is pre-cross but is speaking to the Disciples about the Post-cross life;

> I am giving you my Peace. (sozo)
>> I don't give the way the world gives.
>>> **Don't let yourselves be upset or frightened.**
>>>> You heard me tell you, 'I am leaving,
>>>> and I will come back to you.'

> If you loved me, you would have been
> glad that I am going to the Father;
>
> because the Father is greater than I.
>
> John 14:27

Notice; Don't be upset or frightened Believers can trust the Lord and stay in the peace that Jesus has given you, remember your eternal future is secure. Jesus made a way for mankind to receive right standing with GOD and Jesus has sent the Holy Spirit to be inside every Believer to fulfill Father GOD's plan for the Believers abundant life. GOD's will in Heaven is being done on earth, one Believer at a time.

> Think about the New Creation Born-again life,
>
>> The part of Adam and Eve that died is born-again in Believers.
>>
>> Jesus resurrection made Christians righteous and therefore suitable for the indwelling of the Holy Spirit.
>>
>> The indwelling of the Holy Spirit and power is available for Believers.

The Believer's Spirit has been born-again into the "Image of GOD" and Jesus now holds the keys to death and Hell. Believers have Eternal life and will be blessed by the reflection of their image back to GOD. **The blessings of GOD are not a reward for acts of compassion but are the result of total wellbeing that accompanies being led by the Spirit. Think about the reverse;** The Holy Spirit will not lead you into evil.

STOP! Think about this, Jesus never cast sickness, leprosy, or demons on his crowds, instead through the power of the Holy Spirit Jesus healed all their diseases and cast out all demons. It is a Believers relationship with Jesus that brings and sustains peace, you must claim your inheritance and walk in this relationship with the

Holy Spirit and power to experience the abundant life as promised. Believers who are not living the abundant life and enjoying GODliness must question whether they know what Jesus Christ died to give Believers.

**Your New Creation Spirit
came packed with the
Fruit of the Spirit.**

The Fruit of the Spirit is included in the Believers new creation Spirit, **the fruit of the Spirit is: love, joy, peace, patience, kindness, goodness, meekness, and self-control.** Believers own the fruit of the Spirit, it is yours. The Fruit of the Spirit is available and can be summoned from the Believers Spirit. It is not necessary to pray for God to give you the fruit of the Spirit, the fruit was given with the New Creation Spirit. Listen to the Apostle Paul describe the Fruit of the Spirit:

Galatians 5:22 But the fruit of the Spirit is love, joy, peace, patience, kindness, goodness, faithfulness, gentleness, self-   control; **against such things there is no law.** And those who belong to Christ Jesus have crucified the flesh with its passions and desires.

To effectively use the Fruit of the Spirit, Believers must control your thoughts; A Believer can exchange mourning for joy because there is joy in the Lord. A Believer can exchange anxiety for patience because the answer to our prayers are yes and amen. The Believer can exchange rudeness by others with kindness because your happiness comes from the Lord, not from people.

For Example; For the Believer, who is grossly overweight, the Believer can call on self-control, patience, and other Fruit of the Spirit to capture thoughts and actions that would add to the overweight condition. The Fruit of the Spirit is in Believers, you own it, it is always with you, it works every time. A Believer can call on self-control and by faith, in the Gift of God, know that self-control is within the Believer's authority to control. The choice to do everything in moderation will be successful if you stand against the lust to please your senses and please your GOD.

Another Example; For the Believer who is anxious or depressed, you can call on the promise that you **have not** been given the Spirit of fear but of **love, power and a sound mind**. 2nd Timothy 1:7

A Believers behavior will change, when you know who you are. Carnality is not ordered of the Lord and if you drill down, your spirit is not at peace with the carnal approach to any lust or problem. When a Believer sees or feels your focus moving from Spiritual to carnal, **stop** and change the direction of your thoughts. (Carnality is being led by your senses. Repentance is changing your thoughts or direction.) A Believer is in control of your thoughts to bring them to the Lordship of Jesus Christ. If you are thinking; controlling thoughts might work for Pastors or teachers, but I am bombarded by lustful thoughts, and every time I capture a thought the lust from my senses comes right back, the battle against lusts is a battle but Believers must believe in the authority they have been given and control your thoughts, you own them, they do not own Believers.

Listen to Paul speak to carnality and a Believers response;

> Romans 8:8 Those who are in the flesh **cannot** please God. You, however, are not in the flesh but in the Spirit, **if in fact** the **Spirit of God dwells in you**. Anyone who does not have the Spirit of Christ does not belong to (Jesus) him. But if Christ is in you, although the body is dead because of sin, the Spirit is life because of righteousness. **If the Spirit of him who raised Jesus from the dead dwells in you, he who**

raised Christ Jesus from the dead will also give life to your mortal bodies through his Spirit who dwells in you.

There is power in a Believer baptized in the Holy Spirit because the same spirit that raised Christ from the dead is in Believers. In addition to receiving the Holy Spirit, a Believer is *a child of the King, and has a new Father, Brother, and Friend. The new family brings with it, a new name and the Name of Jesus will give Believers confidence about "Who Believers are." The name of Jesus is the name that is above every name named. When you know "who you are" and "whose you are" Believers are blessed to act in concert with the Holy Spirit and power.*

The Holy Spirit is inside Believers
To reveals GOD's love and gifts.

GOD-centered is not only the desired description of a Believer's focus, but it is a fact, God is centered in the inner sanctum of Believers with the Believers Born-again Spirit. A GOD-centered life is evident when your prayers ask, The Father, **what is on your heart**? What can I do for you today? Does anyone in my family need a kind word or deed? Can I be an answer to a prayer for one of your saints with a word or gift? Lord, help me meet someone I can tell about my relationship with you. The Believer does not need to pray about your daily needs, the Lord knows what you have need for today.

> Matthew 6:31 Therefore do **not** be anxious, saying, 'What shall we eat?' or 'What shall we drink?' or 'What shall we wear?' For the Gentiles seek after all these things, and your heavenly Father knows that you need them all.

Note; It is comforting to know that your Father in Heaven knows what you have need for today. GOD wants you to be prosperous, so you can be a blessing to others. If you are not prosperous then God must use others to bless you. If you listen to the Holy Spirit and conscientiously work, you will be prosperous and have the blessings of the Lord. When a Believer is prosperous they can bless others.

Believers must communicate with the Holy Spirit to affect our lives and the lives of others. Hearing the Holy Spirit is not easy and requires living in the Spirit realm, constantly inquiring of the Holy Spirit about GOD's direction for a Believers thought, circumstances, and direction for your life. Listening constantly, with your heart, mind, and ears for guidance. Here is a TIP, constantly acknowledge God's creation in everything your senses experience. The blessing that you were born or live in America should be praised every minute, you could have been born in poorest part of Africa. The Holy Spirit is constantly broadcasting to Believers, it is necessary for Believers to find the frequency. Believers must practice the presence of the Holy Spirit inside them by constantly talking, praising, listening, worshipping, and prayer. The Holy Spirit will never lead you to covet another spouse, or toward pornography or toward hateful speech but instead the Holy Spirit will lead you to love others more significantly than yourself. Talking to the Holy Spirit does not diminish talking to Jesus or the Father but gives Believers pause to think "What is the most effective way to pray in the Post-Cross era, with the Holy Spirit inside Believers?" In this new era of GOD inside believers.

There are two prayers God will not answer;

> Prayers for things God has already given the Believer, for example, peace or all the Fruit of the Spirit.

> Prayer asking GOD to do something He has given you the authority to do. GOD has given Believers everything necessary for life and GODliness.

Your knowledge of the Bible is mandatory at this point in your prayer life. "What has GOD given you the power to do on Earth?" and "What can the Holy Spirit help you do?" GOD at creation gave mankind all power in the earthly realm. Jesus had to come to Earth as a "man" because God had given mankind all power over everything on the Earth, in the skies, and under the seas, now God has reversed the Garden of Eden betrayal and restored Believers to right standing with God. Believers are God's arms and legs to deliver blessings to those in need. Your destiny is to deliver the blessings of GOD to your family and those in need and live in the arms of a loving GOD.

Are you, as a Believer, treating the Holy Spirit as a "deaf mute"? The Post-Cross life is not all praying to GOD, in Heaven and wanting God to change a circumstance on earth for you, but instead uniting yourself with Almighty GOD, inside you. Believers must constantly communicate with the Holy Spirit for leadership, living power, and understanding of how to use GOD's gifts.

Listen to the Apostle Paul talk about living power;

>1st Corinthians 2:4 And my speech and my preaching *was* not with enticing words of man's wisdom, **but in demonstration of the Spirit and of power: <u>That your faith should not stand in the wisdom of men, but in the power of God.</u>**

GOD does the impossible when we bring the impossible to GOD. The New Creation life with the Holy Spirit is personal to you it is your own experience, GOD is in you. Believers must be in communication with the Holy Spirit to have the demonstration of Spirit and power. God wants to speak and fellowship with Believers and **it is our destiny to act with boldness in the Name of Jesus**. Father GOD is in Heaven with Jesus Christ at His right hand, the Holy Spirit is here with Believers. It is very important for Believers to understand that a relationship with the Holy Spirit enables Believers to use the direction and the power of the gifts of GOD given to Believers here on Earth, now and in this time. Jesus did not do one miracle until the Holy Spirit came on and stayed on Jesus at

His baptism. Believers cannot do miracles from GOD until they are baptized with the Holy Spirit and power.

Listen to Paul in this sermon;

> 1st Corinthians 2:8 None of the rulers of this age understood this, for if they had, they would not have crucified the Lord of glory. But, as it is written,
>
> **"What no eye has seen,**
>
> **nor ear heard,**
>
> **nor the heart of man imagined,**
>
> **what God has prepared**
>
> **for those who love him"**
>
> these things **God has revealed to us (Believers) through the Spirit.**
>
> For the Spirit searches everything,
>
> even the depths of God.
>
> For who knows a person's thoughts
>
> except the spirit of that person,
>
> which is in him?
>
> So **also no one comprehends**
>
> **the thoughts of God except the Spirit of God. Now we have received not the spirit of the world,**
>
> **but the Spirit who is from God,**
>
> **that we might understand**
>
> **the things freely given us by God.**
>
> And **we impart this in words**
>
> <u>not taught by human wisdom</u>
>
> <u>but taught by the Spirit,</u>

interpreting spiritual truths
to those who are spiritual.
The natural person does not accept
the things of the Spirit of God,
for they are folly to him,
and he is not able to understand them
because they are spiritually discerned.

Meditate on these verses what they mean to a Believers life with the Holy Spirit. Read this passage again it is beautiful and powerful.

Jesus in His triumph has sent His Spirit to be in Believers and to reveal the gifts God has given Believers. **This communication from the Holy Spirit can be received from studying God's word, from hearing the word from a Believer, in prayer, or during worship, in meditation, or by audible voice, from your Spirit or in your mind.** The communication of the Holy Spirit will always be in the will of God and will be based in love. It is so important to have enough knowledge of GOD and GOD's word to discern the voracity of the communication Believers receive from the Holy Spirit or a different spirit.

Think about the word Jesus gave to Peter and the difficulty of trust, when it was time to pay their taxes. Jesus said to Peter,

> Matthew17:27 However, not to give offense to them (tax collectors), go to the sea and cast a hook and take the first fish that comes up, and when you open its mouth you will find a shekel. Take that and give it to them for me and for yourself."

Do you believe that Peter had ever found a coin in the mouth of any fish, he had caught, in his entire life as a fisherman? Never, before this experience, but because he had a word from God he went and was successful? What a miracle of provision by God. Do you have enough history with the Holy Spirit to follow his instructions and go fish?

Listen to the Lord talking about speaking to Believers;

> John 10:27 My sheep hear my voice, and I know them, and they follow me: (God is a Spirit)

This scripture is pre-cross, but the scripture is not just dealing with salvation, it is important to the post-cross life with the Holy Spirit, also. Believers must listen to the Holy Spirit and the word of GOD and **speak to the mountains in life** and move those problems into the sea.

Creator God spoke the worlds into existence, Jesus spoke to the waves, demons, and sicknesses, and Jesus taught the disciples to Speak to the mountains and they would move. Believes must speak the ideas and the words from the Holy Spirit to affect the visible world with the power of the Spirit world.

Partaking of the Divine Nature of GOD
Requires Believers to use His promises.

When a Believer unites with the Holy Spirit, and uses the promises of God, you partake of the Divine Nature of GOD. The promises of Jesus and Father God are voice activated.

Listen to this scripture from 2nd Peter 1:3;

> Seeing that **his divine power**
> hath granted unto us **all things**
> **that pertain unto life and godliness,**
> through the knowledge of him that called us
> by his own glory and virtue;
> *whereby he hath granted unto us his precious*
> *and exceeding great promises;*

that through these **ye may become**

partakers of the divine nature,

having escaped from the corruption

that is in the world by lust.

Yea, and for this very cause

adding on your part all diligence,

> **and in your faith supply virtue;**
>
> **and in *your* virtue knowledge;**
>
> **and in *your* knowledge self-control;**
>
> **and in *your* self-control patience;**
>
> **and in *your* patience godliness;**
>
> **and in *your* godliness brotherly kindness;**
>
> **and in *your* brotherly kindness love.**

For if these things are yours and abound,

they make you to be not idle nor unfruitful

unto the knowledge of our Lord Jesus Christ.

For he **that lacketh these things**

is blind, seeing only what is near,

having forgotten the cleansing from his sins.

Notice; God's divine power has granted to Believers "all things" that pertain to life and GODliness, **not sickness and poverty.**

Note; Believers can add diligence, faith, virtue, knowledge, self-control, patience, Godliness, brotherly kindness, and love are yours and will abound to make Believers fruitful. *If we do not have these qualities in our lives, we are blind to the knowledge of GOD just living in the visible world without regard to the Spiritual world that* *controls the visible world. The seen world was created out of the unseen world.* Hebrews 11:3 and 2nd Corinthians 4:18

Are you not confident enough to step out on the word of faith and speak to the mountain in your life and command it to move? The Author is willing to step out on faith and tell all readers that if the Holy Spirit moves you from a heart of compassion to speak to a headache, cancer, demons, or anything else in the name of Jesus Christ, do it. If you don't honor the leading of the Holy Spirit, and someone dies because of fear in your heart of failure, everyone in this story loses. If you acted and were made a fool, it is OK and everyone wins; GOD knows how much you are willing to do for Him and you will learn something about yourself and your relationship with the Holy Spirit, and the person sick saw commitment to the Lord and an act of Love.

Recently in the world's greatest Bible Study, one of our members was struck with ALS and the entire study was devastated as we watched him waste a way to death. The study new Rusty and his passion for the Lord. We prayed for Rusty individually and corporately each week and our prayers were not answered with yes and amen, so what happened? What went wrong, is this a case of bad things happen to good people, and if so where is the scripture? Is this a case of we did not know how to correctly pray for Rusty? Did we ever "speak to the mountain of ALS" and not doubt in our hearts that it "be cast into the sea"? Were we complacent and thought that miracles died with the Apostles and where is the scripture on that fact? I believe the Holy Spirit was nudging me to do something, but I don't know what it was and I did not step out in faith to speak to that mountain and cast it into the sea. This book is born out of my frustration and my realization that I may not have the relationship with the Holy Spirit that I need, and that God wants.

Do you Believe?
or is there a deficit of Trust?

Ask yourself, are **you being led** by the Spirit into pursuit of happiness and fulfillment **or are you dragging the Holy Spirit around in your own carnality?** This question seems rough, but the answer will reveal your focus on fulfilling your lusts and pleasing your senses (self-centeredness) or living and loving life and the GOD, who gave it to you (GOD-centered). If you are a Believer, who has asked GOD for the Holy Spirit, the Holy Spirit is living inside you with your new creation Spirit, that is a fact. That is the "good and the bad news" your every word and action as a Believer is witnessed by the Holy Spirit. Today's question, are you making the Holy Spirit proud?

Listen to "Who you are"? and "whose you are"?
Jesus was the last offering for Sin
  and the only one needed.
    GOD will remember Believers sins no more.
     GOD made your New Spirit righteous.
   Jesus has given Believers a New Spirit and
  Created a Temple inside Believers for the Holy Spirit.
   GOD has sent the Holy Spirit to Believers.
  God abides in Believers in the Temple inside Believers.
    God walks with us
     And talks with us
    Believers are God's People and family.
     Believers have the Fruit of the Spirit.
   The Power of the Holy Spirit is inside Believers.
  The Holy Spirit reveals all the gifts GOD has given Believers.
Are you using the gifts and promises GOD has given to Believers?

God knows what you have need of today. Do you know what GOD desires from you today? If a Believer is plagued with a deficit of trust or compassed about with doubt, a Believer must increase their knowledge of GOD and intimacy with the Holy Spirit to boost confidence in your mind and Spirit? Remember; when in prayer, to ask GOD if he has anything on His mind, "that question" will frame your prayer in the correct position to hear from GOD. GOD knows what you have need of today, do you have any idea what God wants?

Thomas, the disciple, asks Jesus "where are you going and how will we know the way?" Jesus replied that He was the way and then said this,

> John 14:8 Philip said to him, "Lord, show us the Father, and it is enough for us." Jesus said to him, "Have I been with you so long, and you still do not know me, Philip? Whoever has seen me has seen the Father. How can you say, 'Show us the Father'? Do you not believe that I am in the Father and the Father is in me? The words that I say to you I do not speak on my own authority, but **the Father who dwells in me does his works**. Believe me that I am in the Father and the Father is in me, or else believe on account of the works themselves. "Truly, truly, I say to you, **whoever believes in me will also do the works that I do; and greater works than these will he do, because I am going to the Father.**

Do not miss "The Father who dwells in me **does His works**". The Father is in Believers to do His works, the question is; will you offer to be the vessel to do GOD's works? The question is still relevant, "Do you really know Jesus?" "Are you doing greater works than Jesus did?" This may seem like a ridiculous question, but the Bible is without error, so it is important for Believers to stretch our faith to allow GOD to do acts of kindness, that we have not dreamed of doing.

If you are like the author, you do not believe you are doing greater deeds than Jesus did while on earth, but because Jesus went to the Father and sent the Holy Spirit, Believers can expect to do greater miracles then Jesus did. One miracle Believers can do that Jesus, as a man, could not do is tell someone about Jesus sacrifice and opportunity to believe in Jesus and be saved, but the Author is not going to hide behind that miracle. **The era of the Holy Spirit was and is meant to be greater than the era of Jesus Christ because Jesus has joined the Father in Heaven and sent the Holy Spirit with eternal life to Believers.** It is up to Believers to believe the scripture and not alibi our failure to not doubt.

> John 10:27 My sheep hear my voice, and I know them, and they follow me: (God is a Spirit)

This scripture is pre-cross, but the scripture is not just dealing with salvation, it is important to the post-cross life with the Holy Spirit, also. Jesus through the Holy spirit is speaking to Believers.

Have you received The Lord's gift of the Holy Spirit? **Do not live one more second without the Holy Spirit, God's word guarantees that if Believers ask, you will receive the Holy Spirit. Listen to this promise from Jesus;**

> Luke 11:13 If ye then, being evil, know how to give good gifts unto your children: how much more shall *your* heavenly Father **give the Holy Spirit to them that ask him?**

Did you stop and ask the Lord to baptize you with the Holy Spirit, and then thank God for His promise to give you the Holy Spirit? Now start talking to the Holy Spirit, bow your head so you can look at your inner Sanctum where God is abiding with your New Creation Spirit. Start listening to the Holy Spirit with the ears of your heart and mind. Expect the fire of a relationship with a Holy GOD to be all over you. Believe in GOD, His creation, and control of the World; at that point you can live without care, anxiety, and strife. **Believers who don't begin each day with praise, worship and inquiring for direction**

from the Holy Spirit; wake up focused on food, clothing, shelter, family, and the problems they have created for themselves. Letting the cares of the world overtake your schedule will lead to self-centeredness. Depending on GOD must start before the cares of the world lead you to assume your job is to provide your wellbeing from your own power. Always remember and acknowledge that without GOD in control you would not have woken from your sleep.

Listen to these scriptures, describing "who you are" and the promises to back it up. **Believers can control our thoughts and emotions and be led by the Holy Spirit.**

> **John 14:1 Let not your heart be troubled.** You believe in God, believe also in Me.

> **Philippians 4:4 Rejoice in the Lord always,** *and* again I say, Rejoice. Let your moderation (peace) be known unto all men. The Lord *is* near. **Be anxious for nothing,** but in everything by prayer and supplication with thanksgiving, let your requests be made known unto God. And the peace of God, which passes all understanding, shall keep your hearts and minds through Christ Jesus. **Finally, brethren,**

> > **whatever things are true,**

> > **whatever things** *are* **honest,**

> > **whatever things** *are* **just,**

> > **whatever things** *are* **pure,**

> > **whatever things** *are* **lovely,**

> > **whatever things** *are* **of good report,**

> **if** *there is* **any virtue and if** *there is* **any praise, exercise yourselves in these things.**

> **Ephesians 3:14** For this reason I bow my knees before the Father, from whom every family in heaven and on earth is named, <u>that according to the riches of his glory he may grant</u>

you to be strengthened with power through **his Spirit in your inner being**, so that Christ may dwell in your hearts through **faith—that you, being rooted and grounded in love, may have strength to comprehend with all the saints what is the breadth and length and height and depth, and to know the love of Christ that surpasses knowledge, that you may be filled with all the fullness of God. Now to him who is able to do far more abundantly than all that we ask or think, according to the power at work within us,** to him be glory in the church and in Christ Jesus throughout all generations, forever and ever. Amen.

Notice; Believe in GOD, be Anxious for nothing, control your thoughts and finally, now be led by the Holy Spirit who is able to do far more abundantly than all that we ask or think, according to the power at work within Believers.

A Believers inner sanctum has the power to live in victory and reign in life when focused on living life GOD-centered (the opposite of following evil). If a Believer does not talk or listen to the Holy Spirit and does not focus on acting in faith to do good works, the Believer is dragging the Holy Spirit through the Believers mundane day. Once you are born-again and receive the Holy Spirit, the Holy Spirit has no choice but to sit there inside Believers and wait on some act of faith or request, otherwise the Holy Spirit is captive to watch your carnality. GOD will never forsake you, nor leave you, nor force you into anything. Do not be deceived the Holy Spirit is with you convicting you of your righteousness in Jesus Christ, although you may not be listening. The Believer **must choose to live in victory,** GOD wants His will for you, but Father GOD will not override your will.

Believers **can live in thanksgiving,** controlling your mind, and living in GOD's peace, it is up to you. Think about this; Believers are not required to have negative emotions (reaction to a missed goal or displeasure). Believers are designed to act as Stewards, God is the owner, don't allow worldly situations to become personal. Believers are here on earth to do GOD's will. You have authority, but you must command (or be in charge of) **GOD's world.** Believers can be **in control,** the power is inside you, to live in victory through your Spirit in connection with the Holy Spirit.

> **The Holy Spirit** *is living inside Believers and is available to teach the deep things of GOD, reveal the gifts of Christ's inheritance, and act together with the Believers Born-again Spirit according to your authority and power moved by the compassion in your heart. What you do with what you have been given is your choice?*

Let your inspiration grow from these verses in Corinthians about your Spirit and the Holy Spirit; 1st Corinthians 2:9-12.

> But as it is written, …
>> eye has not seen,
>>> nor ear heard,
>>>> neither has entered the heart of man
>> that which God has prepared
> for those that love him.

But God has revealed *this* unto us by his Spirit,
> for the Spirit searches all things,
>> even the deep things of God.
>> For who among men
>>> knows the things of man,
>>> except the spirit of man which is in him?

Even so no one has known the things of God, but the Spirit of God.
> Now we **have not** received the spirit of the world,
>> **but the Spirit which is of God,**

that we might know the things that God

Has given us.

These verses are repeated for emphasis that GOD in the person of the Holy Spirit is inside Believers, **think about that,** are you in communication with the Holy Spirit inside you? Consider the impact of your New Creation Spirit and the Holy Spirit acting together to understand the things GOD has given Believers? If Believers don't ever communicate with the Holy Spirit, you will not know the acts of goodness GOD has for you to do nor the gifts God has given Believers. If you request direction from the Holy Spirit, a word will come to you; it may be from a peace in your heart, or a scripture from your memory, or if the lines of communication seem to be broken read from your Bible and let the word speak to you. If nothing comes through, you may be asking the wrong question or thinking about a distraction from an incorrect angle. Consider, what would GOD want you to do if you had received a word from the scriptures or from the Holy Spirit. When you ask for guidance from the Holy Spirit, you have chosen the right direction and your heart will lead you into an act based on the love that is in your heart.

The Steward's mindset

Believers are GOD's delivery system. Father GOD and Jesus Christ are not coming to Earth to help Believers, because GOD sent his Spirit to be inside you to reign in life, subdue the world, and to multiply physically and spiritually telling everyone about the Gospel of Jesus Christ. The Steward mindset will help Believers focus on delivering the blessings of God to the world. When Believers act on good works, that we are inspired to do; the power and supplies for success will be supplied through the Holy Spirit and GOD's will, will be done.

Listen to Paul in Ephesians1:6-14

To the praise of the glory of his grace, wherein **he hath made us accepted in the beloved.** In whom we have redemption through his blood, the forgiveness of sins, according to the riches of his grace; Wherein he hath abounded toward us in all wisdom and prudence; <u>Having made known unto us the mystery of his **will,** according to his good pleasure which he hath purposed in himself:</u> That in the dispensation of the fulness of times he might gather together in one all things in Christ, both which are in heaven, and which are on earth; *even* in him: **In whom also we have obtained an inheritance,** being predestined according to the purpose of him who worketh all things after the counsel of his own **will: That we should be to the praise of his glory, who first trusted in Christ.** In whom ye also *trusted,* after that ye heard the word of truth, the gospel of your salvation: in whom also **after that ye believed, ye were sealed with that Holy Spirit of promise,** Which is the earnest of our inheritance until the redemption of the purchased possession, unto the praise of his glory.

Notice; Believers are accepted into the beloved. Believers can know your purpose and GOD's will for your actions and Believers are forever sealed in your relationship with God through the Holy Spirit. This scripture is inspiration for the Stewards mindset of caring for others more significantly than yourself.

You are Destiny's child.

At the last supper Jesus gave Believers a new commandment;

> John 13:34 A new commandment I give unto you, that ye love one another; as I have loved you, that ye also love one another. By this shall all *men* know that ye are my disciples, if ye have love one to another.

This verse sets out the destiny for Stewards of GOD's grace. The Spirit of the Lord has set up good works for the Stewards to do and GOD will supply us with everything Stewards need to be successful in their accomplishment. Just like Jesus, Believers must believe that GOD is inside us and that we are "in Him" to form the connection for doing the perfect will of GOD.

Listen to these words from Jesus;

> Act 1:8 But you will receive power when the Holy Spirit has come upon you, and you will be my witnesses in Jerusalem and in all Judea and Samaria, and to the end of the earth."

> Act 1:9 And when he had said these things, as they were looking on, he was lifted up, and a cloud took him out of their sight.

The Lord is no respecter of persons and therefore the power that is resident in the Disciples after the Baptism in the Holy Spirit is in Believers baptized in the Holy Spirit. The Lord gave us the victory in life. To enjoy this victory Believers must grow your relationship with the Holy Spirit. A Believers destiny is filling a need for others from a heart of love for your Savior and that act of kindness allows the Believer to partake of the divine Nature of GOD. *Stewards are powerful and on a mission to listen to GOD and fulfill GOD's will by being in a certain place at a certain time to steward an act that GOD has planned, to answer the prayer of someone. Stewards are the hands and legs GOD uses to fulfill His will and these acts of kindness and supply, through Believers, bring glory to GOD.*

Believers know how to glorify God by good conduct with our bodies but how can we glorify GOD with our Spirit? **The Answer:** Believers must communicate with the God, living inside Believers, communication is the first act of faith. **Thanksgiving, Praise, Worship, and Acts of faith; glorify GOD and reflect God's image back to Heaven. Through communication, Believers acting as stewards, will do acts of kindness that GOD has for you to do.**

Practice speaking to GOD,

> Ask, what does the Holy Spirit want to do or say,

> What can you do for GOD today?

> Take an evil thought captive and cast it away.

> Acknowledge GOD's creation of everything you see;

> light, mountains, oceans, flowers, fruit, food, your life, etc.

> Praise God for what you have and experience,

> Constantly seek intimacy with GOD.

Noted Theologian N. T. Wright describes part of our calling is to be "image bearers", and I agree that after the seeker has been born again in the image of GOD, the daily question for the Believer is image-bearer or self-portrait or Stewardship versus ownership. The Steward of GOD's world will focus on what GOD desires, as differentiated by the pressures of the world to focus on building your own account. The pursuer of ambition and self-interest cannot please GOD, because their focus is divided between two masters. Listen to Hebrews about endurance and steadfastness;

> Hebrews 10:35 Cast not away therefore your confidence, which hath great recompense of reward. For ye have need of endurance (patience), that, after ye have done the will of God, ye might receive the promise.

Do not allow thoughts of failure, but instead harbor thoughts of patience until the success of your mission, prayer or hope. Believers and Stewards have GOD given authority, in life, with the Holy Spirit; there are things to pray about and there is power to speak in the Name of Jesus to change situations and do acts of kindness. Training yourself to hear GOD's voice in your life requires Believers to speak to GOD and listen for GOD's response. The response is there in your mind and in your heart and confirmed by GOD's word. A Believer does not need to pray to GOD about a problem that God has already addressed at the Cross. If GOD or Jesus has given the Believer authority in His word, a Believer needs to speak to the problem about your God, not speak to GOD about the problem.

> Matthew 21:21 Jesus answered and said to them, Truly I say to you, If you have faith and **do not doubt,** you shall not only do *this miracle* of the fig tree, but also; **if you shall say to this mountain, Be moved and be thrown into the sea; it shall be done.**

Advice; A Believer needs to speak to a headache with the power of GOD before you curse cancer and its roots.

Application; Jesus, when he saw leaves but no fruit on the Fig tree, Jesus cursed the Fig tree and the following day when the disciples passed, the Fig tree, it had dried up from the roots. Plants in general die from the leaves down and finally the roots. **Jesus is saying that Believers will be able to do the cursing of the Fig Tree and or the casting of the mountain into the sea, if we do not doubt our authority. This promise must be believed and spoken to change the seen world with the invisible world.**

If you are not casting mountains into the sea, it may be useful to fill up your mind and heart with scriptures. A Believer must obtain more knowledge of GOD than is available at Church one day a week. Your relationship with God, the Holy Spirit, is the most important part of your life and your relationship must be the paramount pursuit; to know about your GOD and your new family. To counter the distracting thoughts of the world; lust, fear, and being void of destiny, Believers must capture the distracting thoughts and refocus on God's word or GOD's creation. One glimpse of the integrity and complexity of the creation of the world and your body will bring your thought life back to your position in the Family of GOD. No one or thing or event can make this world and your body, only God Almighty. A Believers body is living proof of the God of Creation. It takes faith to hear GOD's voice and a Believer must know about God to know what GOD is saying. GOD will never say anything that contradicts His word written in the Bible. The Bible requires constant study, because it is complicated and rewarding with a harvest for all the seeds of love uncovered in it. The underlying focus of a word from GOD will be love, comfort, or peace. **Stretching a Believer's mind, to include GOD, in all your decisions, will affect your actions in a positive way, leading to peace every minute of every day.** This does not mean that you will not have problems to conquer and distractions to overcome but including God will make each decision and action GOD inspired. A Believer's future is secure, and your life is Eternal, therefore you can trust GOD for today. Listen to the beautiful and powerful way that the Apostle Paul describes our status;

God's Everlasting Love

Romans 8:31 What then shall we say to these things?

If God is for us, who can be against us?

He who did not spare his own Son

but gave him up for us all,

how will he not also with him

graciously give us all things?

Who shall bring any charge

against God's elect?

It is God who justifies.

Who is to condemn?

Christ Jesus is the one who died—

more than that, who was raised—

who is at the right hand of God,

who indeed is interceding for us.

Who shall separate us from the love of Christ?
Shall tribulation,
or distress,
or persecution,
or famine,
or nakedness,
or danger,
or sword?
As it is written,
"For your sake we are being killed all the day long;
we are regarded as sheep to be slaughtered."
No, in all these things we are more than conquerors
through him who loved us.
For I am sure that neither death nor life,
nor angels nor rulers,
nor things present
nor things to come,
nor powers,
nor height nor depth,
nor anything else in all creation,
will be able to separate us
from the love of God in Christ Jesus our Lord.

This scripture is the Gospel and is assuring Believers that **nothing can separate a Believer from the Holy Spirit and from the victory of Jesus over evil.**

Homework assignment to do now;

Stop!..... take a moment, ... Archeologists have unearthed the Synagogue at Capernaum where Jesus preached. imagine yourself walking with Jesus in the Synagogue at Capernaum and Jesus is teaching. **Close your eyes,** imagine your clothing and the clothing of Jesus and his disciples, the weather is hot, you are wearing sandals, you are in the synagogue that has been discovered in Capernaum, Jesus is speaking, now relate to this scripture, and see yourself there. Watch and experience, being in the Spirit of GOD.

Jesus Heals a Man with an Unclean Spirit

Mark 1:21 And they went into Capernaum, and immediately on the Sabbath he entered the synagogue and was teaching. And they were astonished at his teaching, **for he taught them as one who had authority,** and not as the scribes. And immediately there was in their synagogue a man with an unclean spirit. And he cried out, "What have you to do with us, Jesus of Nazareth? Have you come to destroy us? I know who you are—the Holy One of God." But Jesus rebuked him, saying, "Be silent, and come out of him!" And the unclean spirit, convulsing him and crying out with a loud voice, came out of him. And they were all amazed, so that they questioned among themselves, saying, "What is this? **A new teaching with authority! He commands even the unclean spirits, and they obey him."** And at once his fame spread everywhere throughout all the surrounding region of Galilee.

Now Close your eyes again, you leave the Synagogue and go to Simon Peter's home just a short walk. Peters mother-in-law has been ill. Now think about entering the house; it has a thatched roof and a dirt or stone floor. Now read on;

Jesus Heals Many

> Mark 1:29 And immediately he left the synagogue and entered the house of Simon and Andrew, with James and John. Now Simon's mother-in-law lay ill with a fever, and immediately they told him about her. And Jesus came and took her by the hand and lifted her up, and the fever left her, and she began to serve them.

Now as the day lingers, all the sick gathered at Simon Peter's home. Imagine that you are helping line up the sick to be healed by Jesus, Scripture says the whole city was at the door. Picture the line and the stretchers and those in agony. Now read on;

> **That evening at sundown they brought to him all who were sick or oppressed by demons.** And the whole city was gathered together at the door. And he healed many who were sick with various diseases, and cast out many demons. And he would not permit the demons to speak, because they knew him.

Now "fast forward" take yourself to the upper room after the Lord's resurrection, Jesus appears in body but comes through the walls and everyone is amazed.

> Luke 24:44 Then Jesus said to them, "These are my words that I spoke to you while I was still with you, that everything written about me in the Law of Moses and the Prophets and the Psalms must be fulfilled." Then he opened their minds to understand the Scriptures, and said to them, "Thus it is written, that the Christ should suffer and on the third day rise from the dead, and that repentance and forgiveness of sins should be proclaimed in his name to all nations, beginning from Jerusalem. You are witnesses of these things. And

behold, I am sending the promise of my Father (the Holy Spirit) upon you. But stay in the city until you are clothed with power from on high."

You are there in the upper room and stay in Jerusalem until you receive the Holy Spirit and power that Jesus has for you. Now open your eyes. Thank God for what you have seen and received.

Listen to the instructions recorded in Acts Given by the Holy Spirit

Listen to these Post-Cross instructions from the Holy Spirit to saints and realize that The Holy Spirit wants to talk to you. Put your-self in these scriptures listening for the Spirit to lead you minute by minute.

These scriptures are individual instructions from the Holy Spirit and not meant to be a continuing story but are pointed out to show "how" the Holy Spirit may lead Believers;

Acts 8:29 **And the Spirit said to** Philip, "Go over and join this chariot."

Acts 9:10 Now there was a disciple at Damascus named Ananias. **The Lord said to him in a vision, "Ananias." And he said, "Here I am, Lord."**

Acts 9:11 And **the Lord said to him,** "Rise and go to the street called Straight, and at the house of Judas look for a man of Tarsus named Saul, for behold, he is praying,

Acts 10:19 And while Peter was pondering the vision, **the Spirit said to him,** "Behold, three men are looking for you.

Acts 10:20 Rise and go down and accompany them without hesitation, **for I have sent them."**

Acts 13:2 While they were worshiping the Lord and fasting, **the Holy Spirit** said, "Set apart for me Barnabas and Saul for the work to which I have called them."

Acts 13:3 Then after fasting and praying they laid their hands on them and sent them off.

Acts 16:6 And they went through the region of Phrygia and Galatia, **having been forbidden by the Holy Spirit to speak the word in Asia.**

Acts 16:7 And when they had come up to Mysia, they attempted to go into Bithynia, **but the Spirit of Jesus did not allow them.**

Acts 17:16 Now while Paul was waiting for them at Athens, **his spirit was provoked within him** as he saw that the city was full of idols.

Acts 18:5 And when Silas and Timotheus were come from Macedonia, **Paul was pressed in the spirit,** and testified to the Jews *that* Jesus *was* Christ (The Messiah).

Acts 20:22 And now, behold, I am going to Jerusalem, **constrained by the Spirit,** not knowing what will happen to me there,

Acts 20:23 **except that the Holy Spirit testifies to me in every city** that imprisonment and afflictions await me.

Acts 21:4 And having sought out the disciples, we stayed there for seven days. **And through the Spirit they were telling Paul** not to go on to Jerusalem.

Acts 21:11 And coming to us, he took Paul's belt and bound his own feet and hands and said, **"Thus says the Holy Spirit,** 'This is how the Jews at Jerusalem will bind the man who owns this belt and deliver him into the hands of the Gentiles.'"

Act 23:11 The following night **the Lord stood by him and said,** As you testified about me in Jerusalem, so you must testify also in Rome."

In addition to these verbal and mental communications from the Holy Spirit, the Apostle Paul tells Believers to set our minds on things in the Spirit and that the Spirit of God will bear witness with our Spirit;

> Romans 8:5 For those who live according to the flesh set their minds on the things of the flesh, **but those who live according to the Spirit set their minds on the things of the Spirit.** For to set the mind on the flesh is death, **but to set the mind on the Spirit is life and peace. The Spirit himself bears witness with our spirit that we are children of God,**

If Believers purpose to be Stewards of GOD's world and focus on caring for others more significantly than our selves the communication, we feel in our Spirit and hear with our heart and ears will be from God through the Holy Spirit.

Listen to God and His word with purpose.

If you don't listen to God who are you going to listen to for guidance.

**Believers are the Temple of the Holy Spirit and
need to live as a living sacrifice.**

Chapter Two

Steward of GOD's Creation
Not an owner of man's accomplishments.

Living in the Spiritual realm and being a Steward for GOD is a new experience for Believers and can be better understood if Believers understand more about creation. God has shown the Believer and the **unbeliever** the truth of Creation through the fulfillment of every sensory aspect of mankind. The Heavens and the Earth can be seen, heard, smelled, tasted, and touched and mankind knows it was created by GOD. GOD as Creator is the beginning of understanding mankind's position in the world in relation to GOD's position. GOD's Creation is the foundation for your faith in God. Listen to this scripture from Romans;

> Romans 1:18 For the wrath of God is revealed from heaven against all ungodliness and unrighteousness of men, who by their unrighteousness **suppress the truth.** For what can be known about God is plain to them, because **God has shown it to *unbelievers*.** For his invisible attributes, namely, his eternal power and divine nature, have been clearly perceived, ever since the creation of the world, **in the things that have been made.** *So unbelievers are without excuse*. For although *unbelievers* knew God, **they did not honor him as God or give thanks to him,** but *unbelievers* became futile in their thinking, and their foolish hearts were darkened. Claiming to be wise, ***unbelievers* became fools,** and exchanged the glory

of the immortal God for images resembling mortal man and birds and animals and creeping things. (as gods)

Notice; "So unbelievers are without excuse." Unbelievers do not honor God or give thanks for the things GOD has made, and therefore unbelievers "became futile in their thinking".

Believers and Stewards honor GOD by acknowledging God's creation and desire to fulfill their purpose to the Creator of All. Most churches concentrate their teaching on Salvation through Jesus Christ which is paramount to the restoring of righteousness to Believers but Salvation or Jesus alone is an incomplete description of our GOD and the mission of Jesus Christ to give the Holy Spirit to Believers. Believers, also, need to know GOD as Creator and as the Holy Spirit to complete our understanding of GOD and move to the New Creation Life with the Holy Spirit. Believers must believe GOD created the visible world to anchor their faith in the invisible world that they cannot see.

> **The era of the Holy Spirit was and is meant to be greater than the era of Jesus Christ because Jesus has joined the Father in Heaven and sent the Holy Spirit with eternal life to Believers.**

Stewardship of the Kingdom of GOD is a Believers purpose, the Believers destiny honors each aspect of the GOD head. Stewardship of God's abundance is the attitude Jesus exhibited when He said, "I have come to serve not to be served."

What is a Steward?

GOD loved **the world**, so much, he gave His son to Believers to save the world and the Son loved mankind so much He has given Believers the Holy Spirit to be inside Believers for peace, guidance, and power. The world is not the Stewards and the purpose of his Stewardship is to bring about the owner's purpose not his own. **The Steward's mindset is humility in the midst of the total authority given the Steward by GOD to rule over the world created by**

God. This humility allows you to rest in the arms of a loving GOD. The humility comes from realizing that Almighty God had a plan for your birth, life, redemption and for Believers purpose to fulfill GOD's will on earth as it is in Heaven. Unfortunately, God's plan only matters if you are a Believer and are talking to God and hearing from the Holy Spirit. The heart of a Steward will act from a motive of respect for the Creator and His goals. The Believers/ Stewards life is concentrated on honoring the Creator and caring for others more than you care for yourself. Just as Jesus has given his life for your redemption. **The Steward mindset is believing that being led by the Holy Spirit for the benefit of others will bring answers to prayers and glory to our Lord.**

The authority for action for Believers is fused with the humility of being a Steward of God's world, not an owner.

> Psalms 24:1 The earth is the LORD's and the fullness thereof, the world and those who dwell therein,

> Psalms 19:1 The heavens declare the glory of God, and the sky above proclaims his handiwork.

Embracing the grandeur of the Heavens and understanding that the Earth belongs to GOD; is the foundation for the gift of authority given the steward. Stewardship is the opposite of slavery; the Steward is in charge of the GOD created world to bring about the instructions of the owner without the responsibilities of ownership.

> **The Golden Rule** started with God when God gave Mankind everything and asked mankind to love God and love our neighbor as ourselves. "Doing unto others as you would have them do unto you".

Stewardship has rewards;

The Bible speaks of five crowns for Believers as one of the rewards for stewardship. These rewards for stewardship are offered after our physical death at the "Bema" seat judgment. This judgement is not a judgement for sin, because sin was judged at the cross and the sin penalty has been paid by Jesus Christ at the cross. The "bema" seat Judgment is for rewards for stewardship.

Hebrews 9:27 And as it is appointed unto men once to die, but after this the judgment:

Adam and Eve died twice, Born-again Believers will only die once because their Spiritual life is eternal, only the body will die. To be prepared for the Rewards Judgement, Believers must focus on building our Spiritual life and intimacy with the Holy Spirit and storing up treasure in Heaven.

In Matthew 6:19 Jesus said,

"Do not lay up for yourselves treasures on earth, where moth and rust destroy and where thieves break in and steal, but lay up for yourselves treasures in heaven, where neither moth nor rust destroys and where thieves do not break in and steal. For where your treasure is, there your heart will be also.

Searching for GOD and the Kingdom must be first, paramount, and constant. Mankind's time on Earth is between 60-120 years, but at the instant of Salvation, a Believer has Eternal Spiritual life. So, live your physical life on Earth to the benefit of your Eternal Spiritual life. "Naked you came into the world and naked you shall leave it", **therefore it is only your accumulation of spiritual accomplishments that matter in your time on earth.** It does not matter how many cars, or houses, or jewelry, or money accumulated. The judgment after death, for Believers, is one of rewards for spiritual accomplishments not a judgment for sin or the amount of wealth attained.

Background; When Adam sinned, it was not that he ate from the tree of sin; He ate from the tree of the knowledge of Good and evil and broke covenant with GOD. For Good and evil to operate in the world, each force needs a body (person); to do good or do evil because GOD gave Mankind all power on the earth, under the sea, and in the air. The Garden of Eden question is each individual's choice to be GOD-centered or Self-centered; the motivation to act with an evil motive or good motives. The question is "Are you an agent for evil or an agent for GOD?" Behavior is only temporary but your belief, in your need for GOD in your life, is the paramount decision leading to eternal life. GOD is interested in the change of the heart, the motivation to believe in Good through belief in Christ's redemption. To make the new Creation life abundant and powerful, God has sent the Holy Spirit to abide with Believers.

Consider the salvation and death of repentant thief on the cross, he did not have any good deeds to his credit, but he has eternal life for his change from "Self-centered to GOD-centered" through belief in Jesus Christ. **This is not the best testimony;** The repentant thief will have the same eternal life as all Believers but at the rewards judgment, the accomplishments of his stewardship purpose were never realized. God had good works of love, for him, to do had the repentant thief had more time to live as an agent for Good. Respecting GOD and listening for God's instructions, allow the Believer to reign in life with the addition of purpose and destiny to do the will of our GOD.

GOD condemned the sin nature and provided Believers with an avenue to partake of GOD's Nature. Romans 8:3

A Believer/Steward can partake of the Divine nature of GOD by using the precious promises granted to Believers through Jesus Christ for the benefit of others. Listen to this beautiful verse from 2nd Peter.

His divine power has granted to us all things

that pertain to life and godliness,

    through the knowledge of him who called us
        to his own glory and excellence,

  by which he has granted to us

his precious and very great promises,

so that through them you may become

<u>partakers of the divine nature,</u>

    having escaped from the corruption

        that is in the world because of sinful
        desire.

  For this very reason, make every effort

to supplement your faith with virtue,

and virtue with knowledge, and

  knowledge with self-control, and

    self-control with steadfastness, and

      steadfastness with godliness, and

   godliness with brotherly affection,

    and brotherly affection with love.

For if these qualities are yours and are
increasing, they keep you from being ineffective or
unfruitful in the knowledge of our Lord Jesus Christ.

For whoever lacks these qualities is so nearsighted

  that he is blind,

    having forgotten

      that he was cleansed

        from his former sins.

Everything needed for the abundant life and GODliness has been given to Believers. It is a fact, that the abundant life and GODliness has been given and the pursuit of this life allows you to partake of GOD's nature. When Believers are using GOD's promises we are partaking of the Divine nature of GOD Almighty. It is an act of faith when Believers talk to God and when we acknowledge GOD's achievement of Creation. When Believers are focused on supplying others in need, (A kind word, an uplifting spirit, time, caring, supporting, ministering the Gospel, etc.) Believers can reflect the image in which we have been made by using the promises of God. GOD will supply everything needed when Believers are being a steward of GOD's abundance, including miracles needed as the Holy Spirit wills. Can you think of a scripture with more impact than being able to partake of the "Divine Nature" of GOD?

If you do not use the precious promises of GOD
You cannot partake of the nature of GOD

Can you name 5 promises you use daily, weekly, or monthly that allow you to partake of God's Divine Nature? And if not make it a priority to start today.

> The Lord is my shepherd and I shall not want. Psalms 23
>
> In Him our prayers are yes and amen. 2nd Corinthians 1:20
>
> My sheep hear my voice. John 10:27
>
> You **have not** been given a spirit of fear, but of love, power and a sound mind. 2nd Timothy 1:7
>
> Preach the Kingdom of GOD and heal the sick. Luke 9:2

These scripture promises are just five examples of over 3,000 Bible promises you can choose for your life. (Remember the inheritance of Jesus Christ's finished works happened at the Cross.) The promises each believer chooses are monumental, if you live them and use them for the benefit of others. To any Believer not fully committed to the belief that God has given Believers authority to reign on Earth; that Believer will live in a "fear of loss mindset" instead of a Stewards mindset of the Lord's power to provide.

Stewards cannot be unbelievers or Self-centered.

The fear of loss mindset is self-centered and leads to idolatry because it chokes out the truth that GOD owns the world and everything in it. Thinking you are in charge, that you own your part of the world, and relying on yourself, as your supplier, will allow fear to rise in your heart. That fear arises when you think your wealth came from your power to get wealth and therefore your loss of assets is your fault. If you have a Stewards mindset and believe that God is the owner of the world, you can bless someone, and you will not lose your wealth because you did not own what you gave away. GOD will replace, with more, any substance GOD tells you to give to someone in need. If Believers do not have a Title Deed **signed by GOD,** then you do not own any part of this world. Anything a Steward gives away, whether it is time, money, or miracles belonged to God and therefore does not take away from the Believers prosperity because the Stewards ability to get wealth is provided by the owner (GOD). Recently in Christian circles, "The prayer of Jabez" was being heralded as a newly discovered reminder of the destiny for Christians.

> **1st Chronicles 4:10** Jabez called upon the God of Israel, saying, "Oh that you would bless me and enlarge my border, and that your hand might be with me, and that you would keep me from harm so that it might not bring me pain!" And God granted what he asked.

Notice; This prayer is a pre-cross prayer of stewardship and there is great news, **the prayer has been answered by Jesus Christ.** In the Post-Cross era of the Holy Spirit; God has enlarged our borders, GOD is abiding with Believers, the spirit of fear has been exchanged for love, power and a sound mind, and Jesus has guaranteed eternal life.

The basis for stewardship is serving a greater purpose than your own. GOD's part of "give and it shall be given good measure pressed down and running over" to the Believers that act on this principle, is guaranteed. This following scripture from Jesus is pre-cross but it is **not** used here to talk about salvation but instead about faith. Give first from a heart of love and you will reap a much larger harvest of gifts from others later.

> Luke 6:38 Give and it shall be given unto you; good measure, pressed down and shaken together and running over, shall men give into your bosom. For with the same measure that ye measure out it shall be measured to you again.

Luke 6:38 is a picture of the Steward's mindset and God's promise; belief that giving of the substance GOD has given you will be replaced with more. When Believers find themselves in need or missing the goal they set, generally GOD was not consulted on the goal. When your heart burns from fellowship with the Lord and you set a goal or get a word in your heart; you will have supply for the goal. Believers are stewards, whether we believe it or not. **Believers not including GOD in their goal-setting stifle their confidence to operate by faith in the supply of GOD to reach their goal.** If a Believer's goals are offered for GOD's blessing and confirmed by the Holy Spirit, there will be supply for the goal. God knows the end from the beginning. Since the beginning of time, the apple seed has produced apple trees and then fruit. GOD's seed is in Believers to produce good fruit and having a Stewards mindset is the attitude that allows grace and truth to be manifested in a Believers life. Confer with the Holy Spirit for goals for each day and for your life so that you can have confidence in the supply for your goals. When an unplanned obstacle happens in your day, ask the Holy Spirit if you are there, at this time, to minister to someone or is this a time to stand against the devil until he flees. The Believer and the Holy Spirit inside you are in charge.

Listen to <u>God's warning to the self-centered.</u> Deuteronomy 8:17-18

> So that you might not say in your heart, **My power and the might of *my* hand** has gotten me this wealth. But you shall remember Jehovah your God, for *it is* He who gives you power to get wealth, so that He may confirm His covenant which He has sworn to your fathers, as it is today.

"Wall Street systems" will not translate to understanding and operating in the systems of GOD's Spiritual Kingdom because the glory for the success goes to man's accomplishment. Service and love for others is not Wall Street's primary motivation. Stewardship is not in their manifesto, they are **not** contemplating GOD's system. Think about these three Godly principles;

> Give and it shall be given unto you.
>
> Forgive others because you have been forgiven.
>
> Do unto others as you would have them do unto you.

Wall Street's focus is driven by the pursuit of the control of things; money, goods, toys, et cetera. **It is the focus of a Believer's purpose** that matters to GOD. If a Wall Street Believers purpose is to make something out of what GOD has given with the mindset to bless others with what you make, then your focus can align with GOD's will. **God wants you to be prosperous, so that you can bless others,** Believers are the only vessel that God has on the Earth to bless others.

Non-believers assume that they happened into this world and they do not credit GOD with creating the world. In the unbeliever's mind, anything unbelievers make with the substance GOD supplied is theirs and they are self-made men and women. Non-believers believe everything they touch, taste, hear, smell, or see happened and they can do with it as they choose. Without understanding it, unbelievers are agents for evil. **Unbelievers are focused on ownership of their world, instead of stewardship of GOD's World.** Every thought that concentrates on the temptations of money and the worlds pleasures instead of stewardship for the Creator of the World, leads to **self-centeredness**.

Self-centeredness is the belief in solving all problems with your own power. Self-centeredness, allowed to grow, leads to replacing GOD Almighty with ambition and setting goals based on fulfilling the pleasure of the senses and self-adulation. This belief in yourself as your god leads to death. Self-centeredness is not based on TRUTH, which is "the evolving of everything to the end of its purpose"; but instead self-centeredness is the introduction of iniquity in the hearts of mankind and leads to death. Listen to this warning from the Apostle Paul;

> Ephesians 4:17-19 This I say therefore, and testify in the Lord, that ye henceforth walk not as other Gentiles walk, *in the vanity of their mind, Having the understanding darkened, being alienated from the life of God through the ignorance that is in them*, because of the blindness of their heart: **Who being past feeling have given themselves over unto lasciviousness, to work all uncleanness with greediness.**

Note; The Self-centered mindset will evolve in to total evil.

Acknowledge GOD
for everything you possess.

The GOD-centered mindset **can be derailed** by forgetting your need for God and His creation and depending on yourself. America offers basic needs with such ease that Believers can find themselves only going to God when you can't solve a problem within your own ability. This assumption that your ability can control your world is a fallacy. Acknowledging God's provision and honoring God as your provider builds a foundation of depending on God, so that when facing a problem without a solution you have GOD with you in your dilemma. A Steward must always give credit to who created his world, who created the supply of all needs, and who redeemed the Believer. If you don't ask God to heal a headache it is difficult to have the faith to believe that God has given you the power to curse cancer and its roots. What is the mountain in your life and do you believe you can speak to the mountain and the mountain would obey you?

Listen to the Apostle Paul again from his teaching of Timothy;

Self-centered or GOD-centered

1Timothy 6 Teach and exhort these things.

If anyone teaches differently,

> and does not consent to sound words,

> > those of our Lord Jesus Christ and the

> > > teaching according to godliness,

> > he has been puffed up,

> > > understanding nothing,

> but *is* sick concerning doubts and arguments,

out of which comes envy, strife, evil-speakings,

> evil suspicions, meddling, of men

> > whose mind has been corrupted and

> > deprived of the truth,

> > > > **supposing gain to be godliness.**

> > > > > Withdraw from such *persons*.

> > > > But Godliness with contentment is great gain.

> > > **For we have brought nothing into the world,**

it is **plain that neither can we carry anything out.**

But having food and clothing, we will <u>be satisfied with these.</u>

But those **purposing to be rich** fall into temptation,

and a snare, and many foolish and hurtful lusts,

<u>which plunge men into ruin and destruction.</u>

For the love of money is a root of all evils,

by means of which some having lusted after *it*

were **seduced from the faith**, and

they themselves pierced through by many pains.

showing the folly, as well as

wickedness of coveting more than

the common necessaries of life;

and **by that humbling truth,**

of bringing nothing into the world,

and the consciousness of carrying nothing out.

It is a similar expression to that of Job.

Naked (said he) came I

out of my mother's womb,

and naked shall I return thither.

Note 1; Those purposing to be rich fall into temptation and lusts that plunge men into ruin and destruction. The great gain comes from **Godliness with contentment. Purposing to be a Steward of GOD's abundance and content with your destiny.**

Note 2; At death, everything Mankind has gained is gone, vanished, of no value. In contrast, the Believer/Steward who has been adding to his or her heavenly account, with acts of kindness, will have rewards on Earth, rewards in Heaven, and Eternal life.

Note 3; A Believer must control their thoughts; envy, strife, evil speaking, meddling are thoughts that must be stopped and brought to the Lordship of Jesus Christ and **Believers have this power and authority to control thoughts and deeds. The Holy Spirit is in you to guide you and join with you in using the authority given to you by Jesus Christ to reign in life.**

Notice; It is the focus of your treasure that determines your motivation; Self-Centered or GOD-centered; owner or steward?

Until a Believer knows GOD's words and they burn in your heart, compassion for others will be masked and a Believer will not fully know his purpose. Have you lived your life to reflect your purpose or do you know your purpose?

Non-believers take credit for the power to get wealth when it was GOD's substance they used in their business and God's power that made the product of their business work. The non-believer is blind.

> **Example;** When asked how you made your fortune? Is your comment, **"I am a self-made man"**?
>
> When asked "What do you want to do after college? Is your comment, **"I want to change the world"**?
>
> When you recite poetry, do you choose, **"I am the Captain of my ship, I am the master of my fate"**?
>
> When your daughter gets engaged, is your first question, **"What kind of job does he have"**?
>
> Is your favorite song, **"My way"**?

In America, it is a very easy step to depend on yourself for your daily food and never enjoy the world GOD made for you. Providing for yourself and family through self-determination and hard work without enjoying a relationship with Creator God is relatively easy but foolish and is fraught with fear. What does a rich man do when he is sick, or his child is addicted to drugs, or needs to know about the salvation offered by Jesus Christ? Money can buy you a house, but it can't make it a home. GOD's creation of the world demands respect because what GOD started at creation is still operating per the instructions GOD set in motion at creation. Believers must not forget who made and controls the world, not out of fear but out of thanksgiving continually being focused on a relationship with GOD.

Stay Focused on GOD.

Believing in the GOD of Creation is essential to living and reigning in the New Creation life focused on doing acts of kindness. You can feel, touch, taste, hear, and see the world God made and wonder at the infinite questions of "How does God determine the tides of the oceans or How did GOD design the fruit trees to be self-propagating"? The sensual ability to experience the world, GOD made, is the beginning basis for faith in GOD. Believers must answer in their hearts, the ownership question, Believers must constantly ask, "What does God want me to do with His creation?" A Believer cannot reflect" Glory" back to GOD without supplying others with substance from GOD's creation and direction. Imagine yourself going into the garden of GOD and picking the fruit of kindness and giving it to someone in need.

Inconveniences and persecutions, in a Steward life, are only distractions, trying to change your focus away from your Lord, who made and controls the world. Any acknowledgment to the distractions of the world is misplaced, because God is in control of the world and eternity. Think about this; Do not speak to God about your distractions **speak to your distractions about your GOD. GOD is in control and inside you and you have been given authority to reign in life.**

Consider these small examples of daily life that are desperately important to you and let them prove that GOD controls the world for your benefit.

Example; Who programmed all the seeds for all the trees and plants each season?

Who programmed the world to spin at 1040 miles per hour?

Do you know, "Who comes, when the earth needs more water or air or rain" or Does the Earth ever need more than the Lord planned at creation?

If the earth needed more air or water what could anyone do to solve the problem? Only GOD can change the world. This statement does not mean that we should not be good stewards of God's earth.

Who made the radio waves that allow your phone to communicate and gravity to keep the satellites in orbit? Motorola and Apple only use what GOD created at creation.

Application

Think about making bread, the baker takes water, leaven, and wheat flour and mixes them together and adds heat and a wonderful smelling and tasting loaf of bread is made. But it was GOD that made the water, the wheat, and the leaven and gave the ingredients the properties to react with each other to make the Bread. **In reality, GOD made it bread.**

When Believers know "Who we are?" and "Where we fit in GOD's world?" it will become easy to live in the humility of "Who GOD is?" and "What our Father has instore for Believers?"

Every day with Jesus
is better than the day before.

Listen to Paul in Philippians 2 sharing the way to Kingdom living;
Humility is the evidence of being a steward.

So if there is any encouragement in Christ,

any comfort from love,

any participation in the Spirit,

any affection and sympathy,

complete my joy

by being of the same mind,

having the same love,

being in full accord and of one mind.

Do nothing from selfish ambition or conceit,

but in humility count others more significant than

yourselves.

Let each of you look not only to his own interests,

but also to the interests of others.

Have this mind among yourselves,

which is yours in Christ Jesus, who,

though he was in the form of God,

did not count equality with God

a thing to be grasped, but emptied himself,

by taking the form of a servant,

being born in the likeness of men.

And being found in human form,

he humbled himself by becoming obedient

to the point of death,

even death on a cross.

Therefore God has highly exalted him and

bestowed on him the name

that is above every name,

so that at the name of Jesus

every knee should bow,

in heaven and on earth

and under the earth, and

every tongue confess that Jesus Christ is Lord,

to the glory of God the Father. Philippians 2

Notice; Do nothing from selfish ambition or conceit, but in humility count others more significant than yourselves.

Philippians 2 is a picture of "the life" a Believer can have and the instructions on how to have this life. When Jesus became obedient to the law and to death on the cross, the curse of the law was eliminated allowing fellowship with God to be restored for Believers.

The mind of Christ is available to Believers through the Holy Spirit when Believers are in full accord and motivated by love.

The Name of Jesus is more than a phrase to put at the end of a prayer, "the name of Jesus" is the power above every name named and is a force greater than anything with a name that at the name of Jesus every Spiritual force must move, both in Heaven and on Earth. Meditate on this name and its power, "the Name of Jesus" is above the name of headache, depression, or cancer. Have you contemplated the importance and power in the name of Jesus and its ranking among words? Do you realize that action in the Spiritual world must be the spoken word in "the name of Jesus"? Remember Jesus is the brother of all Believers and your new family is headed by Father GOD.

Do you want to experience the God of the Bible?

Do you know the blessings that are yours?

Listen to the Blessings offered in the Old Testament to those who will follow the word of the Lord. The blessings still apply.

And all these blessings shall come upon you and overtake you,

> **if you obey the voice of the LORD your God. (and now the voice of the Lord is inside you)**
>
> **Blessed** shall you be in the city, and **blessed** shall you be in the field.
>
> **Blessed** shall be the fruit of your womb and the fruit of your ground and the fruit of your cattle, the increase of your herds and the young of your flock.
>
> **Blessed** shall be your basket and your kneading bowl.
>
> **Blessed** shall you be when you come in, and blessed shall you be when you go out.
>
> "The LORD will cause your enemies who rise against you to be defeated before you. They shall come out against you one way and flee before you seven ways.
>
> The LORD will command the **blessing** on you in your barns and in all that you undertake. And he will bless you in the land that the LORD your God is giving you.
>
> The LORD will establish you as a people holy to himself, as he has sworn to you, if you keep the commandments of the LORD your God and walk in his ways.

And all the peoples of the earth shall see that you are called by the name of the LORD, and they shall be afraid of you. **And the LORD will make you abound in prosperity,**

> in the fruit of your womb and
>
> in the fruit of your livestock and
>
> in the fruit of your ground, within the land that the

LORD swore to your fathers to give you.

The LORD will open to you his good treasury, the heavens, to give the rain to your land in its season and to bless all the work of your hands.

And you shall lend to many nations, but you shall not borrow.

And the LORD will make you the head and not the tail, and you shall only go up and not down, if you obey the commandments of the LORD your God, which I command you today, being careful to do them, and if you do not turn aside from any of the words that I command you today, to the right hand or to the left, **to go after other gods to serve them. Deuteronomy 28:1-14**

These blessings follow on those who stay GOD-centered and not self-centered. This is a Pre-cross promise, but it is not changed with the Post-Cross life offered by the finished works of Jesus at the Cross. The curses that follow in 28:15 were dealt with at the Cross by Jesus being made a curse for Believers and the curses do not pass the grace offered at the cross. Galatians 3:13

Do you understand the Cross?

Think about this; Jesus could have been stoned and His blood covered the Believers sin, stoning was the preferred execution of the Jews but David in Psalm 22:14-16 prophesied that Jesus would be crucified which takes away the curse of the law. Galatians 3:13

At the Cross: The Lord's blood redeemed the Believers sin, His stripes healed our diseases, on the cross he redeemed us from the curse of the law, on His shoulders He bore our sorrows and carried our griefs, He was pierced for our transgressions, His body was bruised for our iniquities, He was punished to bring us peace, and He was made poor that we might become rich. Isaiah 53, Psalms 103, 2nd Corinthians 8:9

All of the finished works of Jesus Christ were accomplished and are all part of the Believers Post-cross inheritance. The power of the New Creation life must be believed and acted on by faith. This power is best activated when Believers use the words of the Bible and "the name of Jesus" in love to do good works. Jesus gave Believers **not** "A measure of faith", but "**the** measure of faith" to every Believer. Romans 12:3. Every Believer has the necessary faith but may need more renewing of their minds to eliminate doubt about their position with GOD. Constantly practice the presence of the Lord.

What can a Believer full of the Holy Spirit **speak with our mouths and believe in our hearts** about the inheritance of the finished works of Jesus Christ? Can you say these words and believe them and if not, what are we to do with the scriptures that say these words?

I have been redeemed by the blood of the lamb.

I was healed by the stripes on Jesus back and live in that promise from Jesus.

Jesus carried my grief and sorrow before it came.

Jesus was pierced to receive my transgressions, so I would not be judged for them.

Jesus was bruised for my iniquities, so I will not be judged for them.

The Lord was punished that I might stay in the peace offered by a loving GOD.

Jesus was made poor that I might be rich.

It is at the Cross that we choose to be God-centered or self-centered. At the Cross, mankind chooses the knowledge of evil or the knowledge of good. After choosing good, a Believers authority and promises, are manifest in the Believers heart and Spirit. The Lord's precious promises are given to Believers who believe and act on what they believe. **A Believer's battle is to believe that GOD has won**

your battle at the Cross and at Creation and a Believer must appropriate or "rest" in the promises and authority given Believers and follow the instructions of the Holy Spirit.

You may be asking, "How do I rest in what GOD did at the cross and at Creation"? The answer is, Believers must fundamentally change the direction of their life from visiting GOD at church a few times a week to living with the Holy Spirit 24 hours a day. As Believers we have the right to be with God all day every day, and your life will be better if you include the Holy Spirit in every decision. Believers can bask in the love of GOD and return love to GOD, this life is available, but Believers must initiate their stream of consciousness toward GOD and away from self-centered thoughts. Believers are in charge of our thoughts.

Your relationship with the Holy Spirit, the compassion of your heart, and your faith will determine how much of Jesus inheritance you know and activate. The new life with the Holy Spirit starts with acknowledging GOD in what you experience with your senses, and actions based on the compassion in a Believer's heart. Remember the admonition, "Do everything in word and deed **all** in "the name of Jesus." **Believers must speak the word and act, all in the Name of Jesus.**

It takes knowledge of GOD to grow your mind to understand the voice of the Lord and to know what to do with the authority and the inheritance that is available for Believers. How are you responding to GOD having won your battles at the Cross; death, hell, and the grave have been conquered? Has your lack of knowledge of what GOD has already finished for you, kept you fighting your battles instead of letting GOD's rod and staff comfort you? Believers must understand that our faith must be in "GOD's grace" not in our actions. A Believers mission is to steward GOD's grace, through a heart of compassion, to those in need. God gave his Son to be crucified that we might have life. **To experience the life given Believers we must speak the accomplishments of our Lord.** God gave His Son first, a free gift, without a requirement of work or payment, but instead as an act of love. The world's problems are not yours, they are the Lord's; Believers must stay "in Christ" resting at the right hand of GOD and walking through this world in victory over our thoughts and emotions telling the world what Jesus has done for Believers and mankind. The Lord has supplied the victory. You can only rest in God's grace, if you are hearing from GOD and His Word. Believers are Eternal Spirits temporarily living in an earthly body. Remember the words from Timothy, "GODliness with contentment".

Let me tell you a story; Once upon a time there was a God, who might have said," these humans are not understanding how to operate in this world and everything I do to help, seems to confuse them. If I were a Human maybe I could communicate with them and show the Humans how to live in this world according to the original intent of sharing the world with them? If I were a human and lived life loving GOD walking perfectly, right in front of them, surely some Humans would see and want to live considering others more significantly than they consider themselves. In that way, love could rule the world as intended at creation. How could I pull that off? What if I took a seed of love and impregnated a willing Woman, and a love child could be born without the baggage of the historical human condition, and after the child lived for a sample period exemplifying service as a way of life. Then if this love child, would sacrifice this part of myself for all who fall short, and create a narrative to change the world for all who would hear this truth and want "love" to rule their lives and the world.

The importance of this story is to look at the Human problem from God's perspective. This is an attempt to think about the problem of evil invading the Human condition and how to restore Humanity. GOD sent a human being to understand, live, and make a way for the Believers to reconciled to God and for Humans to see the love in a world where everyone is more concerned with the welfare of others over themselves.

Stewardship is easy
When we believe GOD is in control.

When Believers realize:
>the God of Creation knew Believers before they were born,
>>That Jesus, redeemed Believers, and
>that the Holy Spirit of God is living in Believers.
>>Believers can then receive the love of GOD
>And because GOD is perfect love,

Believers can bless others giving away GOD's abundance, not theirs.

The only thing GOD gets out of an act of kindness is the satisfaction of seeing a Believer concentrating on a purpose greater than their own. The Believer receives the blessing of being a giver and sowing acts of kindness to God which always brings a harvest. A Believers realization of GOD's World and GOD's plan will foster the confidence and the focus Believers need to reign in life. Sharing the love, we have been given will reflect the image of GOD to our Creator and bring glory to our Redeemer and is every Believers destiny. Listen to this scripture in Hebrews 10:19;

>Therefore, brothers, **since we have confidence to enter the holy places by the blood of Jesus,** by the new and living way that he opened for us through the curtain, that is, through his flesh, and since we have a great (High) priest over the house of God, let us draw near with a true heart in full assurance of faith, with our hearts sprinkled clean from an evil conscience and our bodies washed with pure water. Let

us hold fast the confession of our hope without wavering, for He who promised is faithful. **And let us consider how to stir up one another to love and good works,**

Notice; The scripture says, **"We have" confidence, Believers have this confidence, occasionally** Believers may have been distracted by the lies of the Devil. A believer <u>can wake up this confidence</u> by allowing the Holy Spirit to remind the Believer of the righteousness given to Believers by Jesus Christ at the Cross. Speak the words of the finished works of Jesus that are for Believers.

Meditate on the final admonition; Let Believers consider how to stir up one another to love and good works. (Stewards)

2nd Corinthians 1:20 For the Son of God, Jesus Christ, the one who was proclaimed among you by us, by me and Silvanus and Timothy, did not become "yes" and "no," but has become "yes" in him. For as many as *are the* promises of God, in him *they are* "yes"; therefore also through him *is* the "amen" to the glory of God through us. Now the one who establishes us together with you in Christ and who anoints us *is* God, *who* also sealed us and gave the down payment of the Spirit in our hearts.

STOP; Did you shout when you read this scripture! You do not have to pray for any of the promises of Jesus, the answer is yes and amen!!! These two preceding scriptures show Believers the simplistic beauty of being a Steward and the scriptures give Believers a way to measure the confidence we have in GOD and the power in the Spirit thrilled life. If your measure of "Confidence" is lacking, your knowledge of God's promises is lacking, you know what to do to change that lack. Dedicate yourself to learning more about the promises of GOD and speaking them into the Spiritual world. When Believers study the Bible to learn about your New Creation Life concentrate on scriptures that illuminate the new life in the Holy Spirit. Jesus died, to give Believers the Holy Spirit so that we might live in the new era of the

Holy Spirit. Imagine, part of GOD almighty is living inside you.

The Parable of the three Stewards

GOD has agreed to take care of Believers needs and promotions. The following parable describes the Believers life and promotion according to the stewardship we exhibit. Think about the story of the three stewards;

> Matthew 25:14 "For it will be like a man going on a journey, who called his servants and entrusted to them his property. To one he gave five talents, to another two, to another one, to each according to his ability. Then he went away. He who had received the five talents went at once and traded with them, and he made five talents more. So also he who had the two talents made two talents more. But he who had received the one talent went and dug in the ground and hid his master's money. Now after a long time the master of those servants came and settled accounts with them. And he who had received the five talents came forward, bringing five talents more, saying, 'Master, you delivered to me five talents; here I have made five talents more.' His master said to him, 'Well done, good and faithful servant. **You have been faithful over a little; I will set you over much. Enter into the joy of your master.'** And he also who had the two talents came forward, saying, 'Master, you delivered to me two talents; here I have made two talents more.' His master said to him, 'Well done, good and faithful servant. **You have been faithful over a little; I will set you over much. Enter into the joy of your master.'** He also who had received the one talent came forward, saying, 'Master, I knew you to be a hard man, reaping where you did not sow, and gathering where you scattered no seed, so I was afraid, and I went and hid your talent in the ground. Here you have what is yours.' But his

master answered him, 'You wicked and slothful servant! You knew that I reap where I have not sown and gather where I scattered no seed? Then you ought to have invested my money with the bankers, and at my coming I should have received what was my own with interest. So take the talent from him and give it to him who has the ten talents. **For to everyone who has will more be given, and he will have an abundance.**

A Believers stewardship of God's world will be rewarded, now in this time and in the world to come and the self-centered will have their talents taken from them.

Humans are what they believe and if they don't believe in the God of Creation, Redemption, and the Holy Spirit; they are an unbeliever. Think about this; **GOD did not make Satan the god of this world,** Mankind did, by their belief in self-sufficiency. Mankind has given Satan the power to be the god of this world and the god of their lives. **"You are what you believe."** Satan's world is comprised of pleasing the senses with pride-based actions based on incorrect principles. There is no future in Satan's world, when unbelievers die, there is no eternal life, because Satan cannot prepare for life after human life. Satan is a created spirit, if you follow Satan you will receive his judgment. Death is the consequence of sin and is the vindication of God.

Salvation is the validation of belief in Jesus Christ and is the redemption of GOD. When Jesus died Believers died with Him and when Jesus was resurrected Believers were raised with Him. Jesus in his entire life never brought sickness to any of his encounters with crowds, He never attacked the Pharisees with leprosy, He never sent demons into people. The contrary is the truth of Jesus; He healed the sick, cast out demons, made the leper whole, calmed the sea, raised the dead, made the blind to see, and more. Jesus through the Holy Spirit did not forget to bring health, protection, wholeness, and all that He is when He came to abide in Believers through the Holy

Spirit, but Believers must believe and must not doubt.

The miracles of Jesus and Paul and his fellow Believers flowed from the compassion in their heart for others in need (Steward mentality). GOD's miracles from the Holy Spirit are completely at the behest of the Holy Spirit, but compassion in the heart of a believer is the beginning of the manifestation of miracles. When a Steward has compassion for a situation and can imagine the Lord's solution and a miracle is needed one may be manifest. The most important miracle for a Believer is to help someone find and accept their need for a Savior. A Believers life may be the only sermon an unbeliever may hear. Without Salvation of Jesus Christ, a new Believer cannot experience the powerful life with the Holy Spirit. The importance of Salvation does not diminish the importance of all the finished works of Jesus given to Believers.

**Believers must know who they are
and understand their GOD given authority.**

Believers are part of GOD's family and as Believers we have taken over the family business and need to examine our communication with the Board of Directors (Father GOD, Holy Spirit, and our Brother Jesus Christ). Believers need to be about the Father's business.

<u>Radical change in normal religious thinking</u>.

Our Churches are teaching us to have faith and pray with a desired outcome of moving GOD for a particular need, but that is a Pre-Cross prayer and not possible because GOD is not movable. God is the same yesterday, today and forever. GOD's word is settled. GOD and Jesus both announced that "It is finished" at the end of creation and at redemption. If Jesus and Creator God are finished with their activities, what is next? The answer is; The Holy Spirit. Believers are now inhabited with an eternal Spirit and the Holy Spirit to reign over the visible world with the power of God. What are you doing to increase your relationship with the Holy Spirit?

Do not forget, Jesus died to give the Holy Spirit to abide inside Believers. **Faith does not make GOD move, faith changes the Believer to move ourselves into a position to receive what GOD has provided 2,000 years ago.** God is inside Believers with the Believers Born-again Spirit and it is time for Believers to act like God is with you. Jesus did not forget to bring all of his attributes when He came to abide in Believers through the Holy Spirit.

There are two prayers that **will not** get answered;

>Asking GOD to do something **GOD has already provided.**

>>Love, joy, peace, patience, kindness, goodness, faithfulness, gentleness, self-control;

>Asking GOD to do something **GOD has given you the authority to do.**

For Example;

GOD has given Believers everything necessary for the abundant life and GODliness. Consider the power GOD has given Believers with the Electric Power or Water company, God has given precious promises and instructions for Believers to do, and it is up to Believers to do them. The power company sent power to your house, but you must flip the switch to have power for the light. The water company will not come when you need a drink of water and turn the knob for you. In the same way, GOD is not coming down from His Throne to operate His promises GOD has given you to use. Father GOD and Jesus are "Finished" and now we can join with the Holy Spirit in Jesus Name for provision for the Believers needs and the needs to serve others.

Most prayers are sent to GOD asking GOD to do something He has already provided. Think about your Salvation, it is not the prayer that brings the Salvation, it is the **realization** you need a savior and the **belief** and **acceptance** that Jesus came to Earth to die for your sins and be your GOD that brings Salvation. The "Sinners prayer" should be called the "Believers prayer" because it is affirming the seekers need for a Savior and the change of motivation in your life from Self-centered to GOD-centered, from following the knowledge of evil to a Believer acting with the knowledge of good.

When GOD is at the center of your life, the Believer can look down from the Cross, you share with Jesus, and say to your earthly persecutors,

"Forgive them for they know not what they do."

For example," Think about the **self-centered criminal** crucified with Jesus who said, "If you are the Messiah, save yourself **and us**", and in contrast, think about the other thief who said," Don't you fear God? We deserve the punishment that we are getting but (Jesus) **He has done nothing wrong**". And Jesus remember me when you come into your Kingdom, And Jesus said, "This day will you be with me in paradise." Luke 23:43

Do you see the difference in the actions of Jesus and the repentant thief? Both comments from Jesus and the repentant thief were the words of GOD-centered men, who were reacting to their circumstances from outside their problems, **addressing the circumstances with a Spiritual solution.** Here is a list of emotions and actions **not** given to you by God and you do not have to receive them;

Fear, shame, guilt, revenge, anger, sexual deviancy, bestiality, drunkenness, pride, lust of the eye, etc.

It is the knowledge of God and GOD's Creations that builds faith to say, "The Lord is my shepherd and I shall not want" and believe it.

A Believer is what he or she THINKS
A Believer is not what we think we are.

The motto for a Steward
Do nothing from selfish ambition or conceit, but in humility count others more significant than yourselves.

Notes

Chapter Three

Wisdom from Above
Will not allow strife and demonic influence.

As Stewards, we must constantly check our motives to measure if we are outside the truth of our relationship with the Holy Spirit. If you feel jealousy, strife, or selfishness you are not receiving wisdom from GOD but lies from the enemy. Realize that selfish ambition and bitter jealousy and the impetus to be in strife is demonic. Listen to this verse from James;

> James 3:13 Who is wise and understanding among you? By his good conduct let him show his works in the meekness of wisdom.

> **But if you have bitter jealousy and selfish ambition in your hearts, do not boast and be false to the truth. This (strife) is not the wisdom that comes down from above, but is earthly, unspiritual, demonic.**

> For where jealousy and selfish ambition exist, there will be disorder (strife) and every vile practice.

> **But the wisdom from above**
> **is first pure,**
> **then peaceable, gentle,**
> **open to reason,**
> **full of mercy and good fruits,**
> **impartial and sincere.**
> **And a harvest of righteousness**
> **is sown in peace**
> **by those who make peace.**

Notice the contrast; Anyone whose focus is selfish ambition and jealousy will have a life and attitude based on lies.

Stewards must live on the mountain of victory looking down on the problems of the world from GOD's perspective and employ wisdom from above. Wisdom dissects problems with a focus that is pure, peaceable, gentle, open to reason, full of mercy, impartial, sincere, with good fruits, and is sown in peace. If Stewards consume themselves with the affairs of the flesh or physical world they will not be able to rest in the wisdom of the Holy Spirit. Being a Steward of GOD's world, instead of owner with the owners responsibility, allows Stewards to rest in the power of the Holy Spirit. The unexpected obstacles in life will overwhelm a Steward if you own them and you will default into self-centered ways to take care of the obstacles. Believers must stay connected with the Holy Spirit for guidance to react to all situations and maintain focus on being GOD-centered.

> Consider this; When Believers leave the peace offered by following the Holy Spirit, the result is the Believer becomes dis-eased, not at ease or diseased. The enemy/devil does not want anyone to be at peace with Jesus or at ease with Jesus. All disease is from the enemy.

Self-centered people want to be in the center of the problems or the drama of "who did what to whom", but the Holy Spirit wants to keep you on the mountain of victory and let GOD be in the middle of problems. Do not own problems, remember you are a steward, GOD is the owner; Four examples of what not to do.

> Stewards **will not** have hurt feelings, unless you are in the center of the drama and it isn't going the way you planned.

> When Stewards are in the center of the drama, they are looking for praise for their actions and if praise <u>does not come</u> then everyone is against you.

> Any time Stewards have hurt feelings you are self-centered, and God is not being asked to lead you in your daily activities.

You cannot make a Steward mad without their consent and cooperation.

When you are GOD's steward, your approach to problems will not be driven by pride in what you have done, but in appreciation and humility for what GOD has done. Stewards can walk around without a care, because you cast your care on the Lord, your job as a Steward does not include the responsibilities of the owner.

> 1st Peter 5:6 Humble yourselves therefore under the mighty hand of God, that he may exalt you in due time: Casting all your care upon him; for he careth for you.

GOD is in control of the world He created. Believers know that the Lord is greater than all the distractions in a Believers life, but Believers occasionally forget to use the promises of God and act on their own without direction. Do you believe that GOD wants to be greater than the distractions in your life?

Listen to these statements about our GOD;

GOD **does not** need you to do what he does or has done.

GOD needs you to be **believe who He is** and

What GOD has done and will do through you.

GOD wants the Glory for being your God.

GOD gets no glory out of the works you do without Him.

GOD **does not** need you to be who He is.

You need GOD to be the motivation for who you are.

Every time Believers proceed on a task without a word from the Holy Spirit we do not have the supply for the task from GOD. When Believers operate without a word from the Holy Spirit, we are operating on our own ability and when that happens the supplies for the success of our actions have not been ordered by GOD.

Think about the main subjects of the Bible;

Abraham was told he would be the Father of a great nation but his wife decided she was too old to have children and sent her hand maiden in to sleep with Abraham and the consequence has been a constant acrimony between the Jews and Arabs since that time.

Jacob was told by God that he would be the patriarch above Esau but as Isaac was dying Jacob tricked his father into giving him the blessing GOD had promised Him. This cost Jacob twenty years in slavery to his uncle Laban and the loss of a relationship with his brother.

The Jewish people refused to go into the promised land after leaving Egypt and this caused them forty years of wandering in the desert.

In America, it is easy in this land of plenty, to answer our daily needs with America's abundance. Unfortunately, there are needs that Americas wealth does not hold; sickness, disease, and Eternal life cannot be handled by Americas great monetary wealth. A Believer must be drawing from GOD's wealth and the direction of the Holy Spirit to be ready for obstacles that require a Spiritual solution.

Consider the words of Jesus as He was about to ascend into Heaven;

John 14:12 "Truly, truly, I say to you, whoever believes in me will also do the works that I do; and greater works than these will he do, because I am going to the Father.

The question is; "How do Believers **believe** we can do greater works than Jesus did?" The answer is to duplicate the combination of grace and faith that you as a Believer received from the Holy Spirit to believe in Jesus Christ (even this was a gift). Then accept the fact, Jesus sent the Holy Spirit to be in and on Believers, so GOD could do the works GOD wants to do through Believers. You must meditate on this fact, listen closely, Jesus tells Believers that His Father is doing the acts of miracles through the Holy Spirit. Listen to the words of Jesus in John 14;10-14

Believest thou not that I am in the Father, and the Father in me? the words that I speak unto you I speak not of myself: but the Father that dwelleth in me, he doeth the works. Believe me that I *am* in the Father, and the Father in me: or else believe me for the very works' sake. Verily, verily, I say unto you, He that believeth on me, the works that I do shall he do also; and greater *works* than these shall he do; because I go unto my Father. And whatsoever ye shall ask in my name, that will I do, that the Father may be glorified in the Son. If ye shall ask any thing in my name, I will do *it*.

Believers must unpack the motivation for all actions, twenty-four hours a day and focus on staying GOD-centered and not self-centered. Remember, if your motivation to be GOD-centered loses focus and becomes self-centered the Believer is not assured supply for what is needed for the obstacle of the day. If you want GOD's supply for your Stewardship you must have motivation from the Holy Spirit because the works you are inspired to do, will be done by GOD. (John 14:10) This is very important, God is inside you and when you are united with the Holy Spirit, it is GOD who does the works. Think about your old life, until you became a Believer you were in charge of everything in your life, but now there is a new GOD in your life. Realize that inquiring of the Holy Spirit and what is on the mind of GOD before starting your day allows the Stewards mindset to allow GOD to do his works through you.

Extreme love produces extreme devotion

Suggestion; Love your Father GOD as your Spiritual Father and talk to Him with your appreciation for who and where you are and where GOD is going to take you. As each Believer and the Holy Spirit reign over life and go about doing acts of kindness, the Believer will be thrilled with where you are going. Your prayer life should not be drudgery but should be a love affair.

Understanding Wisdom.
God made wisdom and it is inside you.

Believers are not always in control of your circumstances, but you are always in control of your thinking and your ability to speak to your circumstances. The following Proverb tells Believers about the first creation of GOD which is wisdom. Wisdom is the innate ability for everything in the world to fulfill its destiny. Wisdom is the connection Believers have to operate in the Spirit instead of acting in the flesh. Wisdom is communication to the invisible world and it is through communication with the Holy Spirit that supply for great deeds are accomplished.

Receive Wisdom's instruction,
> rather than <u>silver;</u>
>> **knowledge,** rather than the finest gold.
>>> For **wisdom is better** than pearls;
>> nothing **you want** can compare with Wisdom.
>>> <u>"I, wisdom, live together with caution;</u>
>> <u>I attain knowledge and discretion.</u>

Good advice is mine, and common sense;
> Wisdom is insight, power is mine.
>> By Wisdom do kings reign, and princes
>>> make just laws.

By Wisdom do princes govern, nobles too, and all the earth's rulers.

I (GOD) love those who love Wisdom; and those who seek Wisdom will find me (GOD).
> Riches and honor are with me,
>> lasting wealth and righteousness.

Wisdom's fruit is better than gold, fine gold,
Wisdom's produce better than the finest silver.

Wisdom follows the course of righteousness
along the paths of justice,

to endow with wealth those who love Wisdom
and fill their treasuries.

"GOD made Wisdom as the beginning of his way, "the first" of his ancient works. Wisdom was appointed before the world, before the start, before the earth's beginnings.

When Wisdom was brought forth,
there were no ocean depths,
no springs brimming with water.

Wisdom was brought forth before the hills,
before the mountains had settled in place;

GOD had not yet made the earth, the fields,
or even the earth's first grains of dust.

When GOD established the heavens,
I was there.

When he drew the horizon's circle on the deep,
when GOD set the skies above in place,
when the fountains of the deep poured forth,

when GOD prescribed boundaries for the sea,

so that its water would not transgress his command,
when he marked out the foundations of the earth,

I, Wisdom was with him as someone he could trust.

For me, every day was pure delight,
as Wisdom played
in (GOD's) his presence all the time,

playing everywhere on his earth,

and delighting to be with humankind.

"Therefore, children, listen to me:

happy are those who keep Wisdom's ways.

Hear instruction, and grow wise;

do not refuse it.

How happy the person who listens to Wisdom,

who watches daily at Wisdom's gates

and waits outside my doors.

For he who finds Wisdom finds life and obtains the favor of GOD.

But he who misses Wisdom harms himself;

all who hate Wisdom love death."

Proverbs 8 is written in the Female voice and the author replaced some references to "her" with "wisdom" for emphasis.

Wisdom is the architect and engineer of the characteristics of everything created and its interaction with everything created. GOD through wisdom has issued parameters for everything created and how each individual item would react to every situation.

Examples;

1. **water** plus heat will produce steam,

2. or **a seed planted** in the ground and watered will spring into new life and grow to produce the characteristics of the seed planted according to GOD's design.

Don't get tricked into thinking that you woke up this morning as a self-made man, ready to conquer the world, without GOD to give you air to breathe, energy to move, vision to see, ears to hear, and more.

Without GOD, you could not wake up. As you go to work, think about this fact, everything you use to create wealth was made by God and given its properties of reaction by the wisdom of GOD.

Think about farming;

> **The farmer** can plant a dead seed, and water it, and pull the weeds but the farmer can't make the seed grow, only GOD can program a dried-up "dead" seed and can give it life.

Think about a restaurant;

> **The chef** cannot make any food for the table without animal products made by GOD, or vegetables that cannot be grown without GOD.

> **The baker** can combine ingredients but cannot make any of the seeds that are in the grains, the water, or the leaven necessary for baking.

Think about the weathermen;

> **The weathermen** and women can report what they see or measure temperature and velocity of winds, but they cannot make wind, rain, sunshine, hail, or snow, only GOD controls the elements.

Think about health through Doctors:

> **The doctor** can sew up a cut in your body, but the doctor depends on GOD to make the skin and tissue grow back together.

> **The doctor** can stop your bleeding but depends on GOD for blood transfusions because the doctor cannot make blood.

Notice; The Farmer, Chef, Baker, Weatherman, and Doctor can work with created matter created by God at Creation, but they can't create any new matter. The visible and invisible world is held together by Jesus Christ. Everything that was created, acts and reacts according to the instructions GOD has designed in them. Listen to Apostle Paul describe Jesus;

> Colossians 1:15 He is the image of the invisible God, the firstborn of all creation. **For by him all things were created, in heaven and on earth, visible and invisible,** whether thrones or dominions or rulers or authorities—all things were created through him and for him. And he is before all things, and in Him all things hold together.

The realization that the systems of the world are controlled by GOD, makes being a Steward of what God has made, easy to understand and embrace and gives the Believer faith for believing in the Cross and its benefits.

God so loved the world that he gave the world to mankind as a gift of His love.

> Note; When God gave the world there was no sickness, no thorns, no flesh-eating animals, no evil, and mankind did not have to work by the sweat of his brow.

No matter what vocation a Believer chooses, GOD programmed the underlying product involved in your occupation. God also controls the invisible world that created the visible world. When a Steward understands what GOD has created, it is logical to thank God for everything and credit Him with ownership and work to enact GOD's plan for the distribution of his goodness through stewardship. This act of love or gift of the world from God to mankind is evidence of God's belief in the Golden rule, GOD gave so that we might give to the benefit of others.

Wisdom is the use of **the knowledge of good** to act, speak, or think in the ways of goodness.

Stupidity is the use of **the knowledge of evil** to act, speak or think in the ways of self-indulgence and death.

Listen to Paul in 1st Corinthians speak about wisdom both from an earthly aspect and from the view of God.

> For Jews demand signs and Greeks seek wisdom, but we preach Christ crucified, a stumbling block to Jews and folly to Gentiles, but to those who are called, both Jews and Greeks, **Christ the power of God and the wisdom of God.** For the foolishness of God is wiser than men, and the weakness of God is stronger than men. For consider your calling, brothers: not many of you were wise according to worldly standards, not many were powerful, not many were of noble birth. But God chose what is foolish in the world to shame the wise; God chose what is weak in the world to shame the strong; God chose what is low and despised in the world, even things that are not, to bring to nothing things that are, **so that no human being might boast in the presence of God.** And because of him you are in Christ Jesus, **who became to us wisdom from God,** righteousness and sanctification and redemption, so that, as it is written, "Let the one who boasts, boast in the Lord." 1st Corinthians 22-30

Without God, men can only operate in a sensory knowledge, but Believers operating in Spiritual knowledge that includes Christ who is the wisdom of God can speak to the mountain in your life and it shall move into the sea. If you believe.

The Church has failed Believers in instructing Believers about the Holy Spirit and the Post-Cross life and its power. *Jesus* *faced the same problem of teaching about something that is invisible and described the solution in Matthew;*

> **Matthew 9:1** And getting into a boat he crossed over and came to his own city. And behold, some people brought to him a paralytic, lying on a bed. And when Jesus saw their faith, he said to the paralytic, "Take heart, my son; **your sins are forgiven."** And behold, some of the scribes said to themselves, "This man is blaspheming." But Jesus, knowing their thoughts, said, "Why do you think evil in your hearts? **For which is easier, to say, 'Your sins are forgiven,' or to say, 'Rise and walk'?** But that you may know that the Son of Man has authority on earth to forgive sins"—he then said to the paralytic—"Rise, pick up your bed and go home." And he rose and went home. When the crowds saw it, they were afraid, and they glorified God, who had given such authority to men.

The Pharisees could see the paralytic was healed with their eyes but could not see the working of the Spirit and **would not** have believed that Jesus could forgive sin because it is not visible. In reality, the Pharisees could not believe that Jesus could heal the paralytic, when the Pharisees could see the healing with their own eyes.

In the same way, the Church struggles with the invisible nature of the Spiritual world and the difficulty of teaching about the Holy Spirit because there is no visible evidence. The new creation life starts when Jesus died to give Believers, the Holy Spirit. The Holy Spirit is invisible, and the only evidence is each believer because you cannot come to Jesus without the Holy Spirit draw you. The Church has problems with the Post-cross life Jesus gave Believers because the Holy Spirit is part of God's invisible world. **The fallacy for every Believer is the opposite of the problem Jesus encountered, Believers believe that Jesus forgave our sins which you cannot see and have trouble believing in the healing of the Paralytic which you can see.**

The Church is now in the era of the Holy Spirit but the transference from Jesus Christ in the flesh to the Holy Spirit, who cannot be seen has been difficult. Most churches tear out those pages from the bible or they tell their saints that the baptism of the Holy Spirit is for the time before the Bible was written and now that the Bible is written we do not need the Baptism in the Holy Spirit or miracles, but they could not be more mistaken. **If Almighty God believed Jesus needed the Holy Spirit, it would be stupid for Believers to refuse the Lord's gift of the Holy Spirit for any reason.** The era of the Holy Spirit is one of action for all Believers. Believers have not been trained to use the authority and power in the Believers inheritance primarily because there is no pragmatic evidence of the Spiritual world to the senses.

Therefore, church members without the Holy Spirit, have given their authority over to demonic and evil forces which are stealing, killing, and destroying human lives and our natural environment. **Believers must act in faith, speaking GOD's word to deliver acts of kindness and stand against evil.** Jesus told believers to speak to the mountain, be thou removed into the sea and it would obey. Have you heard a sermon on that scripture? I did not think so. This transference of power to the enemy, is happening because Believers do not know enough about the Holy Spirit living inside Believers to act with boldness to speak to the mountain in your life. Believers are living way below the life God has for them. A Believer can go to church, pray to God, and love GOD and live without the power of connecting with the Holy Spirit. Listen to the Apostle Paul talk about our calling and the power we have to execute God's plan;

> Ephesians 1:17 that the God of our Lord Jesus Christ, the Father of glory, may give you the Spirit of wisdom and of revelation in the knowledge of him, having the eyes of your hearts enlightened, **that you may know what is the hope to which he has called you,** what are the riches of his glorious inheritance in the saints, **and what is the immeasurable**

greatness of his power toward us who believe, according to the working of his great might that he worked in Christ when he raised him from the dead and seated him at his right hand in the heavenly places,

All Believers have a calling and an incredible inheritance of riches and power to accomplish your calling. The calling of God is not necessarily to go somewhere to be a missionary, but universally the calling is to "do unto others as you would have them do unto you." Believers must spend time seeking God so that the Holy Spirit can give you wisdom and revelation of "Who you are." and "Whose you are." The power of the Spiritual world must be spoken to move the visible world with the Truth of the invisible world.

Jesus, through the Holy Spirit, is everything you will let Him be.

Constantly train your mind to see into the Spiritual world,

STOP! Stop Reading and think about looking into the Spiritual world. Now close your eyes and imagine;

The Lord multiplying the fish to feed the five thousand, listen for the Lord having the disciples separate the crowd into 50 and 100-person groups, then the Lord blessed the fish and loaves and the Disciples began to feed the crowd and as they gave away their portion of the five loaves and two fish, all five thousand men and families are fed to their full and there were twelve baskets left over. Notice the Lord's blessing is more than enough. Matthew 14:21

Now imagine; **Watching the words of Jesus** go into Lazarus tomb and energize his body, and see Lazarus hopping out of the tomb wrapped in the linen wrappings. Did you see that, the power moved through His words, "Lazarus come forth" that brought back life to Lazarus, not a prayer but living power of the Holy Spirit through the spoken command. John 11:43

Placing yourself into the settings of the Bible and listening to the compassion of the participants in the early Christian era will help you think about the power of the invisible world of the Spirit.

Consider this scripture from Philippians;

> Philippians 2:13 For it is God which worketh in you both to will and to do of *his* good pleasure.

When a Believer has an image in mind or a word from the Lord you will have the confidence necessary to accomplish good deeds bringing glory to the Lord. If you **haven't** imagined in your mind the basis for an action that Jesus has commissioned for you to do, you will not be successful through the Spiritual world.

> Remember Mark 11:23-4 "Have faith in God.

> Mark 11:23 Truly, I say to you, whoever says to this mountain, 'Be taken up and thrown into the sea,' and does not doubt in his heart, but believes that what he says will come to pass, it will be done for him. Therefore I tell you, whatever you ask in prayer, believe that you have received it, and it will be yours.

If you are not receiving individual communications from the Lord, Believers can still have confidence "to testify to the Gospel of the grace of GOD" as a Believer's appointed mission. Listen to the Apostle Paul;

> Acts 20:24 But I do not account my life of any value nor as precious to myself, **if only I may finish my course and the ministry that I received from the Lord Jesus, to testify to the gospel of the grace of God.**

There is no greater miracle or mission than to testify to an unbeliever about the grace of God and the road to Salvation and welcome a Believer into the Family of GOD, but there is more to the new Creation life. When you can believe in more, more is available. Believers are destined to do the works of Jesus and greater works because Jesus is now with the Father and the Holy Spirit is now with every Believer, who has asked for the Holy Spirit.

Listen to this scripture; your sin is gone past, present, and future.

> **Romans 4:6: "Blessed are those whose lawless deeds are forgiven, and whose sins are covered; blessed is the man against whom the Lord will not count his sin."**

Do not miss; **GOD will not count a Believers sin (past, present, and future).** Do not allow sin conscious teaching of moral standards (daily transgressions) to cloud the only sin that is paramount; the **sin of unbelief** in GOD. For Believers, submerging the Lord's sacrifice in a Believers heart is a picture of the belief necessary for the relationship with GOD to open the doors to His grace. How can a Believer receive this sacrifice of Jesus Christ and not want to please your Savior? The Lord's love will change a Believers desires, words, and actions.

Homework

Add your name to this scripture as a prayer and affirmation of what God has for you. Ephesians 1:17-23

> That the God of our Lord Jesus Christ, the Father of glory, may give **(Your name)** the Spirit of wisdom and of revelation in the knowledge of him, having the eyes of **(Your name)** heart enlightened, that **(Your name)** may know what is the hope to which GOD has called me, what are the riches of his glorious inheritance in the saints, and what is the immeasurable greatness of his power toward **(Your name)**

who believes, according to the working of GOD's great might that GOD worked in Christ when he raised him from the dead and seated him at his right hand in the heavenly places, far above all rule and authority and power and dominion, and above every name that is named, not only in this age but also in the one to come. And he put all things under his feet and gave him as head over all things to the church, which is his body, the fullness of him who fills all in all.

Notes

**If you take matters into your own hands
you take matters out of GOD's hands.**

Chapter Four

Self-Centered or GOD-Centered

Unbelievers, are by their definition, not believers in the God of Creation and redemption, therefore their unbelief defaults into death and idol worship of some kind. Self-righteousness is the belief, you do not need GOD and belief that you or a god of your own making is your great supplier. Any god, mankind makes is by definition only "man-made" and only has man-made power. If you operate from the center of your life instead of from GOD's center you will constantly be in strife and fear.

Believers are by definition Believers in Jesus Christ and are constantly focused on believing more deeply. Believers must do what they know to do concerning a Believers relationship with God. if Believers want to hear from the Holy Spirit for leadership, Believers must learn to communicate with the Holy Spirit. The Holy Spirits promise is to reveal the secret things of GOD that we might understand the things freely given Believers by God. If a Believer is living in adultery or addicted to pornography, it is difficult to use the power of GOD's word or the leading of the Holy Spirit without doubting. When a Believer operates in love there is no defense by the enemy.

The Book of James warns Believer against evil passions ruling your life. Believers need to beware of double mindedness;

Warning Against Worldliness

James 4:1   What causes quarrels and what causes fights among you? Is it not this, that your passions are at war within you? You desire and do not have, so you murder. You covet and cannot obtain, so you fight and quarrel. **You do not have, because you do not ask. You ask and do not receive, because you ask wrongly, to spend it on your passions.** You adulterous people! Do you not know that friendship with the world is enmity with God? Therefore whoever wishes to be a friend of the world makes himself an enemy of God.

The Apostle Paul in Romans proves the indefensible position of unbelievers and the Truth of GOD. Unbelievers worship a created object or thing, instead of the Creator of the world, unbelievers deny there is a creator.

Listen to the Apostle Paul's proof; Romans 1:18

What is revealed is God's anger from heaven

against all the godlessness and

wickedness of people

who in their wickedness

keep suppressing the truth;

because what is known about God is plain to them,

since God has made it plain to them.

For ever since the creation of the universe

his invisible qualities —

both his eternal power
and his divine nature —

have been clearly seen,

because they can be understood

from what (GOD) he has made.

Therefore, unbelievers have no excuse;

because, although they know who God is,

they do not glorify him as God or thank him.

On the contrary,

They have become <u>futile in their thinking</u>;

and their <u>undiscerning hearts</u> have become **darkened.**

Claiming to be wise, they have become fools!

In fact, they have exchanged

the glory of the immortal God

for mere images (idols),

like a mortal human being,

or like birds, animals or reptiles!

This is why God has given them up

to the vileness of their hearts' lusts,

to the shameful misuse of each other's bodies.

They have exchanged the truth of God for falsehood,

by worshipping and serving created things,

rather than the Creator —

praised be GOD (he) forever.

Amen.

Self-righteousness is unbelief and unbelief is "the sin" unto death.

Even for Believers, self-centeredness will lead to futile thinking and block the grace of GOD. Self-centeredness for Believers, can be a temporary position of depending on yourself and not moving toward the goal of GOD's will being done on Earth as it is in heaven. Self-centeredness is the only way to stop GOD's Grace from bringing "Shalom" peace (total fulfillment) to Believers. When a Believers life is not directed by the Holy Spirit you are living under the power of your flesh, and there will not be peace until the Believer can change direction. Changing direction from Self-centered to God-centered can be accomplished in a split second when you realize that you have become centered on your problems instead of centered on your GOD. Listen to Paul in Ephesians talk about a new life with a dedicated purpose;

The priority of a dedicated Mind.

Ephesians 4:17 Now this I say and testify in the Lord,

that you must no longer walk as the Gentiles do,

in the futility of their minds.

They are darkened in their understanding,

alienated from the life of God because of

the ignorance that is in them,

due to their hardness of heart.

They have become callous and have given themselves up to sensuality, greedy to practice every kind of impurity.

But that is not the way you learned Christ!—

assuming that you have heard about him and

were taught in him,

as the truth is in Jesus,

to put **off** your old self,

which belongs to your former manner of life and is corrupt through deceitful desires, and

to be renewed in the spirit of your minds, and to put on

the new self, created after the likeness of God

in true righteousness and holiness.

Therefore, having put away falsehood,

let each one of you speak the truth

with his neighbor, for we are members one of another.

Be angry and do not sin;
 do not let the sun go down on your anger,
  and give no opportunity to the devil.
   Let the thief no longer steal,
    but rather let him labor,
     doing honest work with his own hands,
   so that he may have something to share
  with anyone in need.
Let no corrupting talk come out of your mouths,
 but only such as is good for building up,
  as fits the occasion, that it may give grace
   to those who hear. And
  do not grieve the Holy Spirit of God,
   by whom you were sealed
    for the day of redemption.
   Let all bitterness and wrath and
  anger and clamor and slander
 be put away from you, along with all malice.
Be kind to one another,
 tenderhearted, forgiving one another,
  as God in Christ forgave you.

Stewards must **not** follow the world (senses) but let the world follow the Steward of GOD's grace. Believers must move from any thoughts of self-centered sensuality and greed to put on the new creation life after the image of God. Steward/Believers have the power to subdue the world and that includes controlling all our thoughts and actions. The Steward cannot have two motivators to the Believers action the Steward must be dead to the old sin nature and must be focused on being led by the Holy Spirit. Personal goals in wealth and position must be in concert with the goals for the Believers blessed by GOD for the abundant life and GODliness. The Believer must choose to focus on stewarding God's grace, GOD will supply the wealth and position from His abundance.

Making Christ of no effect
by trusting in Man and his traditions

Examine the following scriptures detailing how a Believer can inhibit the grace and power of the Spiritual Kingdom by being self-centered relying on man's traditional methods of solution. A man-made solution is just that, a man-made solution. Self-centered people will need a GOD made solution at some time in their life and will not know how to communicate to GOD because of the futility of a self-centered life. Listen to these four examples from scripture about falling from grace, and considering the traditions of men or the church more than a word from God.

Galatians 5:3 I testify again to every man who accepts circumcision that he is obligated to keep the whole law. You are severed from Christ, you who would be justified by the law; you have **fallen away from grace.** For through the Spirit, by faith, we ourselves eagerly wait for the hope of righteousness. **For in Christ Jesus neither circumcision nor uncircumcision counts for anything,** but only faith working through love.

Mark 7:6 And he said to them, "Well did Isaiah prophesy of you hypocrites, as it is written, "'This people honors me with their lips, but their heart is far from me; in vain do they worship me, teaching as doctrines the commandments of men.' **You leave the commandment of God and hold to the tradition of men."** And he said to them, "You have a fine way of rejecting the commandment of God in order to establish your tradition!

Hebrews 4:9 So then, there remains a Sabbath rest for the people of God, for whoever has entered God's rest has also rested from his works as God did from his. **Let us therefore strive to enter that rest, so that no one may fall by the same sort of disobedience.** For the word of God is living and active, sharper than any two-edged sword, piercing to the division of soul and of spirit, of joints and of marrow, and **discerning the thoughts and intentions of the heart.** And no creature is hidden from his sight, but all are naked and exposed to the eyes of him to whom we must give account.

Hebrews 12:10 For they verily for a few days chastened *us* after their own pleasure; **but he for *our* profit, that *we* might be partakers of his holiness.** Now no chastening for the present seemeth to be joyous, but grievous: nevertheless afterward it yieldeth the peaceable fruit of righteousness unto them which are exercised thereby. Wherefore lift up the hands which hang down, and the feeble knees; And make straight paths for your feet, lest that which is lame be turned out of the way; but let it rather be healed. Follow peace with all *men,* and holiness, without which no man shall see the Lord: **Looking diligently lest any man fail of the grace of God; lest any root of bitterness springing up trouble *you,* and thereby many be defiled;**

Believers must stay in constant communication with the Holy Spirit to stand against the wiles of the enemy and prevent hardness of the heart through doubt. To develop and deepen a relationship with the Holy Spirit a Believer must talk to the Holy Spirit about anything and everything and listen with intensity for the right thing to do. **When**

you think you don't hear anything from GOD, your mind will draw on the knowledge of GOD in your heart and the Holy Spirit will remind you of scriptures or GOD's love or will give you peace for the course you have chosen. If you are striving to do what God would have you do in any situation, you are on the right track.

Beware of the enemy's devices. The Devil is constantly trying to influence Believers to believe badly about yourself, as the devil feels badly about himself. Lucifer was the most beautiful creature that God made until the curse when he was changed to a serpent crawling on the ground. The devil wants mankind to feel the shame he felt. The Devil wants you to feel inferior, guilty, and ashamed. Rejection is a tool from the enemy, thoughts that Believers are a flawed person, but those thoughts are a lie of the Devil, and are WRONG.

Believers are born-again in the image of God. **The Spirit of God never condemns the forgiven.** The writings of Paul define, for Believers, the "Post Cross" life with the Holy Spirit. **We are judged on the condition of our Spirit, not our actions.** Hebrews 12:22-23 A Believer's Spirit has been made perfect by Jesus. Think about being made perfect by Jesus, "How can this be?" Your born-again Spirit is made perfect and cannot be tarnished by sin. You either have a born-again Spirit or you do not.

Walk with God in whatever vocation or position of the world that you are given. Don't be tempted to brag on yourself but understand your position in the universe of GOD and constantly acknowledge the stature of your GOD. **You are all that GOD is in you. Believers should have an excellent demeanor for it will lead to promotion.**

Pride is believing in your own power.
Shame is believing in the value,

the Devil and his lies have assigned you.

A prideful man is self-centered, and GOD centered man is a humble. Listen to these words from Peter about humility;

> 1Peter 5:5 .... Further, all of you should clothe yourselves in **humility** toward one another, because God opposes the arrogant, but to the **humble** he gives grace. Therefore, **humble** yourselves under the mighty hand of God, so that at the right time he may lift you up. **Throw all your anxieties upon him, because he cares about you.** Stay sober, stay alert! <u>Your enemy, the Adversary, stalks about like a roaring lion looking for someone to devour.</u> **Stand against him,** firm in your trust, knowing that your brothers throughout the world are going through the same kinds of suffering. You will have to suffer only a little while; after that, God, who is full of grace, the one who called you to his eternal glory in union with the Messiah, will himself restore, establish and strengthen you and make you firm. To him be the power forever and ever. Amen.

Self-centered life	GOD Centered life
Success is pleasing your senses and lusts.	Success is pleasing GOD and doing good.
Belief in yourself as being in charge creates accountability to always succeed.	Belief that we are born into God's Creation. And living in Stewardship of GOD's world.
Pride is a result of individual success, intelligence, or good looks and deteriorates.	There is no condemnation to those who are born again.
Success, when failing from stubbornness, dishonesty, pride, or disease, results in destructive emotions of guilt and shame.	Repentance reorients the steward and destroys guilt and an excellent demeanor leads to promotion.
Guilt is feeling bad about what you have done, driven to succeed in your own eyes, at the expense of family and friends.	GOD gives mercy, instead of what is deserved. God gives grace, which is good when you deserved judgement.
Shame is feeling bad about who you are because of what you have become and what you stand for as a person.	GOD comforts his children. GOD is love and the opposite of evil. GOD hates pride, arrogance and evil ways.
Death is the end.	Death is just the beginning.

Believers who find themselves acting self-centered make Christ of no effect in their lives, Self-centered Believers block the grace from Jesus by depending on themselves. Servant leadership or the Stewards mindset opens the avenues to the grace of GOD by depending on God's word and serving others. **Think about this; the Steward mindset of thinking about others more highly than you think of yourself will build a great marriage and will develop great children.**

Satan is trying to destroy your worth

GOD has given Mankind enormous authority and power in the world and to GOD's dismay Believers and unbelievers have been coerced through the lust of the eye, the lust of the flesh, and the pride of life to relinquish their power to non-human spirits and evil powers in high places for momentary pleasures.

> Mat 12:34 You brood of vipers! How can you speak good, when you are evil? **For out of the abundance of the heart the mouth speaks.** The good person out of his good treasure brings forth good, and **the evil person out of his evil treasure brings forth evil.**

Mankind has allowed the lust for the pleasures of the senses to rule over man, but Jesus came and offered mankind power over these demonic influences through the power of the Spiritual world. Look at the Believers authority given by God;

> Matthew 10:1 And he called to him his twelve disciples and gave them authority over unclean spirits, to cast them out, and to heal every disease and every affliction.

> Luke 10:19 Behold, I have given you authority to tread on serpents and scorpions, and over all the power of the enemy, and nothing shall hurt you. Nevertheless, do not rejoice in this, that the spirits are subject to you, but rejoice that your names are written in heaven."

> James 4:7 Submit yourselves therefore to God. Resist the

devil, and he will flee from you. Draw near to God, and he will draw near to you. Cleanse your hands, you sinners, and purify your hearts, **you double-minded.**

If Believers don't renew their minds with the word of GOD and stay in communication with the Holy Spirit, Believers can go back and forth from Self-centered to GOD-centered, but there is a better way. Listen to this scripture from James about the end result of the double minded lifestyle.

James 3:14   But if you have bitter jealousy and selfish ambition in your hearts, do not boast and be false to the truth. This **is not** the wisdom that comes down from above, but is earthly, unspiritual, demonic. For where jealousy and selfish ambition exist, there will be disorder and every vile practice.

Believers can control your emotions.
And correct wrong thinking.

Emotions are the result of feelings from pain or pleasure, but **emotions are a part of the curse** because they are **not founded on the truth,** but on outside circumstances. Emotions are like being blown about by the wind; happy and then sad, one way and then the other way. Emotions can default into guilt and shame and that leads to depression and death. The root of negative emotions is a sense of powerlessness over your life. **Do not allow emotional decisions (powerlessness) to control your actions.**

Believers must recognize negative emotions and react with **GOD's word** or your thoughts will turn to anger and then condemnation leading to hopelessness. Believers can control our thoughts and not react to emotions because we know our purpose and our GOD and his word. Believers when led by the Holy Spirit and God's word are secure in their relationship with God and their eternal future. Your day will be a success because you accomplished what the Holy Spirit inspired you to do, not disappointed because you did not do what your old flesh would have done.

The Believer gives thanks "in" all situations, but not "for" all situations.

> When you have a flat tire, a Believer may have a chance to witness to someone in need, or if you help someone with a flat tire and miss an appointment you may get to witness or answer a prayer for the driver with the flat. Either circumstance can disrupt your plans and upset you, if you are in charge, but the flat can be God's providence if you are a Steward, the disruption will **not** upset you because your time is not your own but is GOD's.

> Believers by concentrating on their eternal life and connection with the Holy Spirit avoid the momentary problems, lusts, and circumstances. Remember lust is personal.

>> 2nd Corinthians 4:15 For it is all for your sake, so that as grace extends to more and more people it may increase thanksgiving, to the glory of God. So we do not lose heart. Though our outer self is wasting away, **our inner self is being renewed day by day.** For this light momentary affliction is preparing for us an eternal weight of glory beyond all comparison, **as we look not to the things that are seen but to the things that are unseen.** For the things that are seen are transient, but the things that are unseen are eternal.

Did you see? Believer/ Stewards must look at the spiritual world, not the circumstances in front of you. It is your motivation for your life and actions that matters to GOD.

Spiritual world and Physical world

The road to destruction is paved with self-centered people who have forgotten GOD. The following Chapter from Isaiah is a Pre-cross Chapter and the penalty for sin is not applicable but the actions that lead Believers into being Self-centered actions will cause the hardening of the heart and that will make it more difficult to appropriate God's grace and promises.

> Isaiah 59:1 Behold, the LORD's hand is not shortened, that it cannot save, or his ear dull, that it cannot hear; but your iniquities have made a separation between you and your God, and your sins have hidden his face from you so that he does not hear. For your hands are defiled with blood and your fingers with iniquity; your lips have spoken lies; your tongue mutters wickedness. No one enters suit justly; no one goes to law honestly; they rely on empty pleas, they speak lies, they conceive mischief and give birth to iniquity. They hatch adders' eggs; they weave the spider's web; he who eats their eggs dies, and from one that is crushed a viper is hatched. Their webs will not serve as clothing; men will not cover themselves with what they make. Their works are works of iniquity, and deeds of violence are in their hands. Their feet run to evil, and they are swift to shed innocent blood; their thoughts are thoughts of Iniquity; desolation and destruction are in their highways. The way of peace they do not know, and there is no justice in their paths; they have made their roads crooked; no one who treads on them knows peace. Therefore, justice is far from us, and righteousness does not overtake us; we hope for light, and behold, darkness, and for brightness, but we walk in gloom. We grope for the wall like the blind; we grope like those who have no eyes; we stumble at noon as in the twilight, among those in full vigor we are like dead men. We all growl like bears; we moan and moan like doves; we hope for justice, but there is none; for

salvation, but it is far from us. For our transgressions are multiplied before you, and our sins testify against us; for our transgressions are with us, and we know our iniquities: transgressing, and denying the LORD, and turning back from following our God, speaking oppression and revolt, conceiving and uttering from the heart lying words.

Judgment and Redemption

Justice is turned back, and righteousness stands far away; for truth has stumbled in the public squares, and uprightness cannot enter. Truth is lacking, and he who departs from evil makes himself a prey. The LORD saw it, and it displeased him that there was no justice. He saw that there was no man, and wondered that there was no one to intercede; then his own arm brought him salvation, and his righteousness upheld him. He put on righteousness as a breastplate, and a helmet of salvation on his head; he put on garments of vengeance for clothing, and wrapped himself in zeal as a cloak. According to their deeds, so will he repay, wrath to his adversaries, repayment to his enemies; to the coastlands he will render repayment.

So, they shall fear the name of the LORD from the west, and his glory from the rising of the sun; for he will come like a rushing stream, which the wind of the LORD drives. ***"And a Redeemer will come to Zion, to those in Jacob who turn from transgression," declares the LORD. "And as for me, this is my covenant with them," says the LORD: "My Spirit that is upon you, and my words that I have put in your mouth, shall not depart out of your mouth, or out of the mouth of your offspring, or out of the mouth of your children's offspring," says the LORD, "from this time forth and forevermore."***

Before the grace offered by Jesus Christ for the way to Salvation was impossible for flawed people to attain but after the Cross there is a better way, but it is the choice of every person to choose God or to go their own way. Eternal life or destruction? Jesus came to deliver Believers from this present evil age; and bring Believers into the era of the Holy Spirit.

Listen to the Apostle Paul;

> Galatians 1:3 Grace to you and peace from God our Father and the Lord Jesus Christ, who gave himself for our sins **to deliver us from the present evil age,** according to the will of our God and Father, to whom be the glory forever and ever. Amen.

Notice; Jesus came to deliver Believers from this present evil age. Believers have been given fellowship with God through the indwelling of the Holy Spirit. The enemy has been defeated and Believers are the victors through Jesus Christ and are now righteous in the sight of God. A Believers testimony of redemption by Christ Jesus is the victory over the lure to be self-centered and the Believers destiny to be GOD-centered.

> Concentrate on "Casting your cares on Him because He cares for you" 1ˢᵗ Peter 5:7

Believe in God's provision and don't be burdened with thoughts of your need for food, clothing, and a place to stay but instead seek first the Kingdom of GOD and the Lord's righteousness. GOD knows what you have need of for today.

Bless the Lord, O My Soul

Notice; the focus or direction of your heart is either with GOD or following your carnality or senses. Listen to these three excerpts from Psalms identifying what GOD offers those who choose to love and follow GOD;

> **Psalms 103:1 Of David.** Bless the LORD, (*This instruction*

is a command, Bless the Lord, said to David's mind, will, and emotions.) O my soul, and all that is within me, bless his holy name! Bless the LORD, O my soul, and **forget not all his benefits,** who forgives all your iniquity, who heals all your diseases, who redeems your life from the pit, who crowns you with steadfast love and mercy, who satisfies you with good so that your youth is renewed like the eagle's.

Psalms 103:8 The LORD works righteousness and justice for all who are oppressed. He made known his ways to Moses, his acts to the people of Israel. The LORD is merciful and gracious, slow to anger and abounding in steadfast love. He will not always chide, nor will he keep his anger forever. **He (GOD) does not deal with us according to our sins, nor repay us according to our iniquities.** For as high as the heavens are above the earth, so great is his steadfast love toward those who fear him; as far as the east is from the west, so far does he remove our transgressions from us. As a father shows compassion to his children, so the LORD shows compassion to those who fear (reverence) him.

Psalms 103:14 For he knows our frame; he remembers that we are dust. As for man, his days are like grass; he flourishes like a flower of the field; for the wind passes over it, and it is gone, and its place knows it no more. **But the steadfast love of the LORD is from everlasting to everlasting on those who fear him, and his righteousness to children's children, to those who keep his covenant and remember to do his commandments.**

GOD is love and the opposite of evil. GOD hates pride, arrogance, evil and duplicitous speech.

Pride is believing your important

in the grand scheme of things, unfortunately,

you are not important, but Believers are important to GOD.

Think about what you can do that is absolutely new.

Can you create anything without using something God made?

The answer is **no,** you cannot make anything new.

But making something new is not your job.

GOD is available to speak to His Children
Speaking to GOD confirmed in the Bible

Do you believe that God will talk or communicate to you? Jesus says His followers know His voice, the Holy Spirit is inside Believers to communicate with Believers and teach Believers the deep things of GOD, talking to GOD and hearing from GOD cannot be manifest if Believers do not believe that God wants to speak to you. Below are transcripts of conversations between Abraham, Moses, and God Almighty. These conversations were between friends not just a top down conversation from God.

Abraham Intercedes for Sodom with GOD

Abraham and GOD;

Genesis 18:22 So the men turned from there and went toward Sodom, but Abraham still stood before the LORD. Then Abraham drew near and said,

Abraham speaking to GOD

"Will you indeed sweep away the righteous with the wicked? Suppose there are fifty righteous within the city. Will you then sweep away the place and not spare it for the fifty righteous who are in it? Far be it from you to do such a thing, to put the righteous to death with the wicked, so that the righteous fare as the wicked! Far be that from you! Shall not the Judge of all the earth do what is just?" And the LORD said,

GOD speaking to Abraham

"If I find at Sodom fifty righteous in the city, I will spare the whole place for their sake."

Abraham answered and said, "Behold, I have undertaken to speak to the Lord, I who am but dust and ashes. Suppose five of the fifty righteous are lacking. Will you destroy the whole city for lack of five?"

GOD speaking to Abraham

And he said, "I will not destroy it if I find forty-five there." Again he spoke to him and said, "Suppose forty are found there." **Abraham answered,**

GOD speaking to Abraham

"For the sake of forty I will not do it." Then **Abraham said,** "Oh let not the Lord be angry, and I will speak. Suppose thirty are found there." **Abraham answered,**

GOD speaking to Abraham

"I will not do it, if I find thirty there." **Abraham said,** "Behold, I have undertaken to speak to the Lord. Suppose twenty are found there." **Abraham answered,**

GOD speaking to Abraham

"For the sake of twenty I will not destroy it." Then **Abraham said,** "Oh let not the Lord be angry, and I will speak again but this once. Suppose ten are found there." He answered,

God speaking to Abraham

"For the sake of ten I will not destroy it." And the LORD went his way, when he had finished speaking to Abraham, and Abraham returned to his place.

Moses and GOD Exodus 19
Negotiating with GOD

Exodus 32:6 And they rose up early the next day and offered burnt offerings and brought peace offerings. And the people sat down to eat and drink and rose up to play.

And the LORD said to Moses,

> **"Go down, for your people, whom you brought up out of -the land of Egypt, have corrupted themselves.** They have turned aside quickly out of the way that I commanded them. They have made for themselves a golden calf and have worshiped it and sacrificed to it and said, 'These are your gods, O Israel, who brought you up out of the land of Egypt!'"

And the LORD said to Moses,

> **"I have seen this people, and behold, it is a stiff-necked people. Now therefore let me alone, that my wrath may burn hot against them and I may consume them, <u>in order that I may make a great nation of you."</u>**

But Moses implored the LORD his God and said,

> "O LORD, why does your wrath burn hot against your people, whom you have brought out of the land of Egypt with great power and with a mighty hand? Why should the Egyptians say, 'With evil intent did he bring them out, to kill them in the mountains and to consume them from the face of the earth'? Turn from your burning anger and relent from this disaster against your people. Remember Abraham, Isaac, and Israel, your servants, to whom you swore by your own self, and said to them, 'I will multiply your offspring as the stars of heaven, and all this land that I have promised I will give to your

offspring, and they shall inherit it forever.'"

And the LORD relented

from the disaster that he had spoken of bringing on his people. Then Moses turned and went down from the mountain with the two tablets of the testimony in his hand, tablets that were written on both sides; on the front and on the back they were written. Exodus 32:16 The tablets were the work of God, and the writing was the writing of God, engraved on the tablets. When Joshua heard the noise of the people as they shouted, he said to Moses, "There is a noise of war in the camp." But he said, "It is not the sound of shouting for victory, or the sound of the cry of defeat, but the sound of singing that I hear." And as soon as he came near the camp and saw the calf and the dancing, Moses' anger burned hot, and he threw the tablets out of his hands and broke them at the foot of the mountain. He took the calf that they had made and burned it with fire and ground it to powder and scattered it on the water and made the people of Israel drink it.

And Moses said to Aaron,

"What did this people do to you that you have brought such a great sin upon them?"

And Aaron said,

"Let not the anger of my Lord burn hot. You know the people, that they are set on evil.

For they said to me, 'Make us gods who shall go before us. As for this Moses, the man who brought us up out of the land of Egypt, **we do not know what has become of him.**

Aaron said to Moses

' So I said to them, 'Let any who have gold take it off.' So they gave it to me, and I threw it into the fire, and out came this calf." And when Moses saw that the people had broken loose (for Aaron had let them break loose, to the derision of their enemies), then Moses stood in the gate of the camp and said,

Moses to those who had not worshipped the Golden Calf

"Who is on the LORD's side? Come to me." And all the sons of Levi gathered around him. And he said to them, "Thus says the LORD God of Israel, 'Put your sword on your side each of you, and go to and fro from gate to gate throughout the camp, and each of you kill his brother and his companion and his neighbor.'" **And the sons of Levi did according to the word of Moses. And that day about three thousand men of the people fell.**

Moses to the Levites

And Moses said, "Today you have been ordained for the service of the LORD, each one at the cost of his son and of his brother, so that he might bestow a blessing upon you this day." The next day Moses said to the people, "You have sinned a great sin. And now I will go up to the LORD; perhaps I can make atonement for your sin.

Moses to GOD

" So Moses returned to the LORD and said, "Alas, this people has sinned a great sin. They have made for themselves gods of gold. **But now, if you will forgive their sin**—but if not, <u>please blot me out of your book that you have written."</u>

But the LORD said to Moses,

"Whoever has sinned against me, I will blot out of my book. But now go, lead the people to the place about which I have spoken to you; behold, my angel shall go before you. Nevertheless, in the day when I visit, I will visit their sin upon them." **Then the LORD sent a plague on the people, because they made the calf, the one that Aaron made.**

Pre-cross

This day when the tablets of the law were delivered 3,000 Israelites who bowed their knee to worship the golden calf died.

Post-cross

The day after the Holy Spirit fell on the upper room at Jerusalem at the first sermon of the Apostle Peter 3,000 people were saved.

The Holy Spirit wants to communicate with Believers

What are you doing to cultivate a communicating relationship with the Holy Spirit? Every book in the Bible screams out that the Lord loves his people and that he wants to communicate with you. He wants to walk with you and talk to you and be your Father and for you to be His child. There are many instances of the Holy Spirit speaking to the early church members all through Acts of the apostles.

Develop for yourself a group of questions to ask GOD that will spur answers or debate;

> Father, Do you have anything on your heart for me today?

> Father, do you want me to bless someone today with your love, time, or money?

> Holy Spirit, I do not understand how to use the inheritance Jesus has left me? Can you help me find scriptures and or speak to me about this?

Then there are situations like a flat tire which seems to happen at a bad time, and you can ask Holy Spirit, "am I here to speak to someone about GOD or our Lord Jesus Christ?" Or Holy Spirit are you leading me away from where I was going?

> Your child is facing a trial and you might ask, "Shall I deliver my child out of this problem with some money or scriptures or is he learning to fly on his own and he will call if I am needed?

You and the Holy Spirit are a team, huddle up and call a play from
God's playbook.

Understanding the origin of sin.

Chapter Five

Wrong believing will ruin your life.

The beginning of the Story of Mankind gives Believers one of the keys to living in the Kingdom of GOD. What does the scripture mean when it is said their eyes were open and they knew they were naked, ashamed, and hid from GOD? We know their eyes were open from creation. Believers are being taught something; What is it?

Right believing would have stopped Lucifer in his tracks, "Did GOD really say" and "GOD knows your eyes will be opened and you shall be as gods" and "you will know good and evil". The same thinking that Jesus used in the temptation needed to be used in this temptation of Adam and Eve, "man shall not live by bread but **by every word that proceeds out from God" This statement would have stopped Lucifer in his tracks. Now let us look at the Garden experience.**

The Garden of Eden

Lucifer was not Satan in the Garden of Eden "until iniquity was found in his heart", Lucifer was a Special Angel who was perfect in beauty and was sent to minister to Adam and Eve with music and more. Listen to the description of Lucifer and what pride in his own beauty cost him.

> Ezekiel 28:12 …Thus says the Lord GOD: **"You were the signet of perfection, full of wisdom and perfect in beauty.** You were in Eden, the garden of God; every precious stone was your covering, sardius, topaz, and diamond, beryl, onyx, and jasper, sapphire, emerald, and carbuncle; and crafted in gold were your settings and your engravings. On the day that you were created they were prepared. **You were an anointed**

guardian cherub. I placed you; you were on the holy mountain of God; in the midst of the stones of fire you walked. **You were blameless in your ways from the day you were created, <u>till unrighteousness was found in you.</u>**

Notice; Lucifer was and is a spirit and does not have a human body. He was an angel.

Notice; Lucifer was in the Garden to minister to Adam and Eve.

<u>**Now we learn about the fall of Lucifer**</u>.

> O guardian cherub, from the midst of the stones of fire.

> Ezekiel 28:17 Your heart **was proud because of your beauty; you corrupted your wisdom for the sake of your splendor.** How art thou fallen from heaven, O Lucifer, son of the morning! *how* art thou cut down to the ground, which didst weaken the nations!

> Isaiah 14:11 **Thy pomp (pride) is brought down to the grave,** *and* the noise of thy viols (beautiful instruments): the worm is spread under thee, and the worms cover thee. <u>For thou hast said in thine heart, I will ascend into heaven, **I will exalt my throne above the stars of God:** I will sit also upon the mount of the congregation, in the sides of the north: I will ascend above the heights of the clouds; I will be like the most High.</u>

And Adam and Eve's eyes were opened and they knew they were naked and they were ashamed. Their physical eyes were already open, so what is the scripture really saying?

Now their eyes were open to evil and self-centered leadership and resisting being led by GOD. At the moment of realization that disobedience to God was their decision and it exposed their choice to break covenant; and cost Adam, Eve, and Lucifer a relationship with GOD.

Listen to the scripture revealing iniquity in the heart of Lucifer and his deceit to Eve to question GOD's word:

> **Genesis 3:1** Now the serpent (Lucifer) was more astute than all the animals of the field which the LORD God had made. And he said unto the woman, Has God indeed said, Ye shall not eat of every tree of the garden?
>
> Genesis 3:2 And the woman answered unto the serpent, We may eat of the fruit of the trees of the garden;
>
> Genesis 3:3 but of the fruit of the tree which *is* in the midst of the garden, God has said, Ye shall not eat of it; <u>neither shall ye touch it, lest ye die.</u>

This is not what God told Adam, *God said, "Do not eat of the tree"*

> Genesis 3:4 Then the serpent said unto the woman, Ye **shall not surely die:**

Note; and Lucifer probably convinced Eve to touch the fruit and she did not die and she concluded that Satan was correct.

> Genesis 3:5 For God knows that in the day ye eat of it **then your eyes shall be opened,** and ye shall be as gods, knowing good and evil.

The devil is always lying with shades of truth, Adam and Eve were already like GOD. The word "knowing" used here is intimacy with good and with evil.

> Genesis 3:6 And **when the woman saw** that the tree *was* good for food, and that it *was* desirable to the eyes, and a tree of covetousness to understand, she took of its fruit and ate and gave also unto her husband with her; and he ate.

Eve believed the lie of the devil and not the word from GOD.

Genesis 3:7 **And the eyes of them both were opened,** and they knew that they *were* naked; so they sewed fig leaves together and made themselves girdles.

Genesis 3:8 And they heard the voice of the LORD God walking in the garden in the cool of the day, and the man and his wife hid themselves from the presence of the LORD God among the trees of the garden.

Lucifer was not a serpent or snake, until iniquity was found in his heart or until GOD cursed Lucifer and **gave him a new name,** "Serpent" GOD said, from this day forward you will crawl in the dirt. Until that time Lucifer stood upright.

Genesis 3:14 The LORD God said to the serpent, "Because you have done this, cursed are you above all livestock and above all beasts of the field; **on your belly you shall go, and dust you shall eat all the days of your life.** I will put enmity between you and the woman, and between your offspring and her offspring; he shall bruise your head, and you shall bruise his heel."

Everyone has the choice to use free will to believe in GOD or believe in yourself as your god. Salvation is dependent on belief in God as creator, redeemer, and friend.

The Question: Can Believers refrain from eating the lies of the Devil? Let us examine what happened to Adam, Eve, and Lucifer. What happened to degrade Lucifer to be Satan? To eliminate suspense, it was pride, but let us look further.

It is from the iniquity in Lucifer's heart that the questions posed to Eve were shaped to build aspirations and lust, in Eve, to be like GOD, when she was already like GOD. She believed the lie from the deceiver.

God's command; **Genesis 2:16** to Adam, "You may surely

eat of every tree of the garden, but of the tree of the knowledge of good and evil you shall not eat, for in the day that you eat of it you shall surely die."

Satan's question to Eve; He said to the woman, "Did God actually say, 'You shall not eat of any tree in the garden'?"

The woman said to the serpent, "We may eat of the fruit of the trees in the garden, but God said, 'You shall not eat of the fruit of the tree that is in the midst of the garden, **neither shall you touch it,** lest you die.'" *Touching it was not said to Adam."*

But the serpent said to the woman, "You will not surely die. (the authors addition is you will not die if you touch it) For God knows that when you eat of it your eyes will be opened, and you will be like God, knowing good and evil." **Their eyes were already open and** *they were already like GOD.*

So when the woman saw (Author's addition that she could touch it and not die) that the tree was good for food, and that it was a delight to the eyes, and that the tree was to be desired to make one wise, she took of its fruit and ate, and she also gave some to her husband who was with her, and he ate.

And now iniquity was found in the heart of Mankind.

Immediately the Eternal Spirit connection with GOD was dead and they knew they were naked and they were ashamed, and Adam and Eve hid from GOD and mankind needed a Savior. Their eyes were open to seeing the evil they had committed and feeling the shame that comes with committing evil and the death of their relationship with GOD.

The Tree of Life is available.
Do not miss this connection to Jesus Christ.

God placed two Angels to guard the Tree of Life so that Adam and

Eve could not eat of that tree and be in a sinful state forever. **GOD then started his plan to have the "Tree of Life" replanted in the era of the Holy Spirit so that all Believers in Jesus Christ could partake of the Tree of Life in the midst of the Garden of Eden and become eternal.** The tree of life is Jesus Christ.

Mankind needed a Savior.

Now receive the Lord's gift of the Holy Spirit to teach Believers, about the gifts, GOD has for those who believe. A Believers covenant with GOD was given and must be accepted at the Cross approximately 2,000 years ago. Understanding that Jesus, "finished" payment for all sin and created righteousness for all Believers, "Once for all time" is difficult to understand but it is a fact. GOD set up the plan for restoring mankind's relationship with God when God said,

> The LORD GOD said to the serpent, "Because you have done this, cursed are you above all livestock and above all beasts of the field; on your belly you shall go, and dust you shall eat all the days of your life. I will put enmity between you and the woman, and between your offspring and her offspring; **he shall bruise your head, and you shall bruise his heel."** Genesis 3:14-15

This is the first mention of a redemption plan by GOD. The need in a Believers heart to change the direction of their life and follow GOD is the key to "reversing intimacy with evil" and to restore right standing with GOD Almighty.

> "God so loved **this world** He sent his only Son that **whosoever believeth** on Jesus would not perish but have everlasting life."

Being GOD-centered has its foundation on believing in Creation of the worlds by God. **Therefore GOD,** and GOD only, has the ability to set in motion the plan for the redemption of mankind and GOD's world. Creator GOD, after creating the universe, said, "it is finished".

Jesus after his sacrifice said, "it is finished" fulfilling every requirement of the law necessary to pay for the entire universe of sin and restore righteousness to all believers.

> Jesus will never have to come back to the cross to die for sin. Creator GOD will never have to return to plant another tree, make more water, or air.

Understanding that the past, present, and future of GOD's promises at creation and redemption are finished and stored up for Believers is critical to Believers accessing them. It is vital for Believers to understand how to appropriate the finished works of Jesus. How do Believers get understanding of the authority given to Believers at the Cross and at Creation through the abiding of the Holy Spirit with Believers? **Very important, Believers cannot appropriate with their faith anything that the Grace of GOD has not already produced. You cannot have faith for another man's wife, or for favor with a bank you want to rob, or a pink Cadillac. The Lord's sacrifice and GOD's creation has given Believers, redemption, sanctification, the fruit of the Spirit, health for our bodies, the gift of the Holy Spirit, and power over the invisible world.**

Upon the foundation of GOD as creator of all, Believers can build faith in God from experiencing and acknowledging God for everything a Believer sees with your eyes, touches with your hands, hears with your ears, tastes with your mouth, and smells with your nose. Everything Believers experience, has its beginning in GOD, a Believer must believe GOD said, "Let there be light, and light was *created*" to have a basis for believing, "Whosoever believeth in Jesus Christ shall have everlasting life". It is the belief in God, His Son, and the Holy Spirit and a Believers need for GOD that makes God's grace available. At this point in your relationship with GOD, the Believers faith in God's grace will appropriate the gifts of GOD given to Believers.

What is the logic for GOD's plan for the world and redemption of mankind? To the worldly brain there is no logic in God's plan, but God's plan is easy to understand if you start with the foundation of Creation of the worlds by GOD. In the beginning, GOD created the Garden of Eden, a habitat created out of perfect love. This Garden was planted by God to supply Mankind with everything they needed in their life and in addition a relationship with Almighty God. Every evening GOD joined Adam and Eve for a walk in the Garden. The importance of this walk with God is that GOD is a Spirit and Adam and Eve were in the human world and could see into the Spiritual world because there was no sin in the hearts of Adam and Eve. God wanted Human kind to live forever, never die, never age, but Adam and Eve abandoned GOD's will and chose to be an agent for evil. The difference between Mankind and all the other creatures in the world is mankind has a free will to choose what they do with their lives and loves. The battle in the Garden was a spiritual battle and God and mankind lost. At the point of disobedience, mankind's DNA changed, and part of mankind's relationship with the Spiritual world ended.

GOD had a plan for redemption of the dead part of Mankind and put it into action. The plan for Believers was redemption through a man living the law and instructions of GOD perfectly. Jesus was that man. Jesus could not be raised from the dead until mankind was redeemed and justice was satisfied for mankind's choice to leave God's will. Belief in Jesus changes Believer's lives and restores their righteousness. Now salvation depends on Jesus instead of mankind. Jesus is the Tree of Life and when we partake of Jesus Christ Believers are eternal. If Believers had not been acquitted, then Jesus would still be dead, and mankind would be dead in their sins. 1st Corinthians 15:1-17

The Holy Spirit is your receipt that justice for your sin has been paid-in-full. Resurrection is not the payment for your sin. Resurrection is evidence that the Spiritual world is greater than the world you can see.

Genesis 1:27 So God created man in his own image, in the image of God he created him; male and female he created them. And God blessed them. And God said to them, "Be fruitful and multiply and fill the earth and subdue it, and have dominion over the fish of the sea and over the birds of the heavens and over every living thing that moves on the earth." And God said, "Behold, I have given you every plant yielding seed that is on the face of all the earth, and every tree with seed in its fruit. You shall have them for food. And to every beast of the earth and to every bird of the heavens and to everything that creeps on the earth, everything that has the breath of life, I have given every green plant for food." And it was so.

GOD created man and gave him authority over every created thing on the earth or in the air and under the waters. Jesus operated in the world according to the old covenant and the law of Moses. After Resurrection, Jesus set in motion the new covenant and the "Post Cross world" with the gift of the Holy Spirit, sin no longer rules mankind or the earth and the Believers authority was restored with the reborn right standing with GOD. Through their own choice Believers reversed Adam and Eve's choosing intimacy with evil. Everything given by Jesus at Calvary was accomplished 2,000 ago. Believers must appropriate the promises of GOD by belief in the Spiritual world and the power of a righteous Believer, joined with the Holy Spirit to reign in life.

The promises available in the inheritance Jesus gave the Saints for "Acts of kindness" in the Spiritual world include; salvation, redemption, healing, peace, prosperity and more. Believers must know what promises are included in their inheritance and know how to write a check on or act on their inheritance.

If you are unable to imagine the invisible world of the Spirit, consider God's underpinning of all the physical items you can see, touch, taste, hear, or smell; the world of atoms, molecules, and gravity. The visible world was spoken into existence by the word of GOD.

> Hebrews 11:3 By faith we understand that the universe was created by the word of God, so that **what is seen was not made out of things that are visible.**

The atomic, molecular, DNA, and gravitational parts of our world are invisible and absolutely designed by GOD for the operation of our world. Stop and imagine seeing gravity or the atoms moving at atomic speed inside the chair you are sitting on. Realize it is Jesus Christ that controls the atoms to do what they were designed to do, so that the chair will support you. Believers, **not unbelievers,** are made in the image of God and given the authority over this world by our Creator. When the Godhead said, "Let us make man in our image." It was the Spirit of Adam and Eve that was made in the image of GOD, because GOD is a Spirit. When a Believer receives his "Born again Spirit" the Believer will never sin again because there is no law from which to be judged because Jesus fulfilled the law. Without the law there is no sin against the law. Jesus "made" your born-again Spirit righteous and perfect. This does not mean that we love our GOD with all our heart and love our neighbors as we love ourselves, but the God question is, "Do you believe you need a God in your life and if so do you believe in the sacrifice of Jesus to restore your covenant with GOD and reunite yourself with the Family of GOD.

The destiny and purpose of Believers is to produce a harvest of treasure from the seed of love planted in you by Jesus Christ. The spiritual question is "How can Believers change our mind, will, and emotions to depending on the word of GOD, and intimacy with the Holy Spirit to access the grace of the Spiritual world and not live by our senses?" Self-centered or GOD-centered, agent for evil or agent for good, that is the question? A Believers relationship grows from worshipping and thanking God for the world, the Savior, the Holy

Spirit, the flowers, the heavens, the oceans, our families, the Bible, our lives and more.

Become God-centered
You cannot serve two masters.

When Believers realize we needed GOD and chose to go from self-centered to GOD-centered our old habits of the flesh did not disappear, and old habits are **not** easy to change. It takes learning about GOD and his words to change the content of your heart. Changes in a Believers heart will change your behavior. Receiving the love of Jesus in our hearts through the belief in your need for a savior, changes a Believers desires. Listen to the Mother of Jesus when she found a word from God. In the face of death for being found pregnant with a child, Mary said to GOD's messenger, "Behold I am a servant of the Lord, **may it be unto me according to your word** ". **Can Believers say the same? This Holy Spirit is inside you, "asking you to follow"; will you say, "May it be to me according to your word".**

Listen to Paul from the letter to Colossae.

> If then you have been raised with Christ, seek the things that are above, where Christ is, seated at the right hand of God. **Set your minds on things that are above, not on things that are on earth.** For you have died, and your life is hidden with Christ in God. When Christ who is your life appears, then you also will appear with him in glory. Put to death therefore what is earthly in you: sexual immorality, impurity, passion, evil desire, and covetousness, which is idolatry. On account of these the wrath of God is coming. **In these you too once walked, when you were living in them.** But now you must put them all away: anger, wrath, malice, slander, and obscene talk from your mouth. Do not lie to one another,

seeing that you **have put off the old self with its practices and have put on the new self, which is being renewed in knowledge after the image of its creator.** Here there is not Greek and Jew, circumcised and uncircumcised, barbarian, Scythian, slave, free; but Christ is all, and in all. **Put on then, as God's chosen ones, holy and beloved, compassionate hearts, kindness, humility, meekness, and patience, bearing with one another** and, if one has a complaint against another, forgiving each other; as the Lord has forgiven you, so you also must forgive. **And above all these put on love, which binds everything together in perfect harmony.** And let the peace of Christ rule in your hearts, to which indeed you were called in one body. And be thankful. **Let the word of Christ dwell in you richly, teaching and admonishing one another in all wisdom, singing psalms and hymns and spiritual songs, with thankfulness in your hearts to God.** *And whatever you do, in word or deed, do everything in the name of the Lord Jesus, giving thanks to God the Father through him.* Colossians 3

Meditate on the last sentence from Colossians 3, "What does it mean to do everything in word or deed do all in the Name of Jesus Christ"? The largest fear Christians face is that GOD won't deliver his promise for you, but GOD has already delivered if you are a Believer. The Believer must now communicate with the Holy Spirit to act on the grace that has been given at creation and at the Cross. Every provision for life and Godliness has been provided at the Cross and at Creation, the Believer must appropriate the finished works by faith and in joint effort with the Holy Spirit.

Listen to the Apostle Paul talk about living power,

> **2Timothy 1:6** For this reason I say to you, <u>Let that grace of God which is in you, given to you by my hands, have living power</u>. **For God did not give us a spirit of fear,** <u>but of</u> **power** <u>and of</u> **love** <u>and of</u> **self-control**. Have no feeling of

shame, then, for the witness of our Lord or for me, his prisoner: but undergo all things for the good news in the measure of the power of God; Who gave us salvation, **marking us out for his purpose,** <u>not on account of our works, but in the measure of his purpose and his grace</u>, which was given to us in Christ Jesus before times eternal, But has now been made clear by the revelation of our Savior Christ Jesus, who put an end to death and made life unending come to light through the good news,

Again, meditate on the promises God installed in your heart with your Born-again Spirit, **"GOD gave Believers; power, love, and self-control."** Think about the Paul's words, **"Let the grace of GOD which is in you have living power".** You have this grace in your Spirit, it is yours to call on when needed.

Your salvation was paid for 2,000 years ago and a Believer must reach in to the Spiritual world to appropriate Salvation and all the gifts of GOD with our faith through love, and the word of GOD. GOD created the world, delivered Mankind's redemption, and has sealed us into our eternal lives by sending the Holy Spirit to indwell us. **Can you believe** in the God of Creation that supplies you with the world, which you can see, feel, and touch; and Jesus Christ and the Holy Spirit who supply you with salvation and all the promises which you can't see?

Believers must understand that God acted first and gave his Son who provided Believers with everything pertaining to life and Godliness. Believers can frustrate the flow of GOD's grace by acting in GOD's position. A Believers trust in GOD will be tested? Can a Believer's thought life stay focused on acknowledging the great things in your world and thinking of others more than you think about yourself? To see if your trust is still in money and self-sufficiency?

Answer these questions; Are you a giver or a hoarder? Are you speaking to and hearing from the Holy Spirit?

GOD does not need your help but desires your trust, if you trust GOD he will supply your existence allowing you to commune with Him and go about doing acts of kindness. **God gave Believers this world and redeemed Believers from your sin, you are blessed, to be a blessing. Take this scripture to heart it is your new covenant;**

> Hebrews 10:10 And by that will **we have been sanctified through the offering of the body of Jesus Christ once for all**. And every priest stands daily at his service, offering repeatedly the same sacrifices, which can **never take away sins.** But when Christ had offered <u>for all time a single sacrifice for sins, he sat down at the right hand of God,</u> waiting from that time until his enemies should be made a footstool for his feet. **For by a single offering he has perfected for all time those who are being sanctified.** And the Holy Spirit also bears witness to us; for after saying, **"This is the covenant that I will make with them after those days, declares the Lord: I will put my laws on their hearts, and write them on their minds," then he adds, "I will remember their sins and their lawless deeds no more." Where there is forgiveness of these, there is no longer any offering for sin.**

Meditate on this; Jesus has perfected you for all time! The law is written in your heart. The Holy Spirit is in your heart.

> Philippians 2:1 Do nothing in your own power, do everything in the name of Jesus.

GOD <u>made</u> your "born-again" Spirit <u>righteous</u>.

Jesus <u>made</u> your Spirit <u>righteous</u> so that the Holy Spirit could live with your Spirit in the inner sanctum of your body.

> Romans 5:17 For if, because of one man's trespass, death reigned through that one man, **much more will those who receive the abundance of grace and the free gift of righteousness reign in life through the one man Jesus Christ.** <u>Therefore, as one trespass led to condemnation for all men, so one act of righteousness leads to justification and life for all men.</u> **For as by the one man's disobedience the many were <u>made sinners,</u> so by the one man's obedience the many will be <u>made righteous.</u>** Now the law came in to increase the trespass, but where sin increased, grace abounded all the more, so that, as sin reigned in death, **grace also might reign through righteousness leading to eternal life through Jesus Christ our Lord.**

You do not have to die to experience your eternal life, your eternal life was sitting at the foot of the cross waiting for Believers nearly 2,000 years ago. The full effect of Eternal life will have impediments until we focus on living in the Spirit and not existing in the flesh. Father GOD wants to take care of His children, the question is; can you find the confidence in God so that you might rest in "the peace" offered by GOD, the complete wellbeing of GOD's family.

> 2nd Corinthians 10:5 tells us," Bring every thought captive to the Lordship of Jesus Christ." When your thought-life is brought to the Lordship of Jesus Christ, you will know which thoughts to keep and which to throw away.

The Pharisees when they realized they had killed the Messiah asked Peter, "What shall we do?"

> Acts 2:36 Let all the house of Israel therefore know for certain that God has made him both Lord and (Messiah) Christ, this Jesus whom you crucified." Now when they (Pharisees) heard

this they were **cut to the heart,** and said to Peter and the rest of the apostles, "Brothers, <u>what shall we do?</u>" **And Peter said to them, "Repent (meaning to change your mind about Jesus being the Messiah) and be baptized every one of you in the name of Jesus Christ for the forgiveness of your sins, and you will receive the gift of the Holy Spirit.** For the promise is for you and for your children and for all who are far off, everyone whom the Lord our God calls to himself." And with many other words he bore witness and continued to exhort them, saying, "Save yourselves from this crooked generation." So those who **received his word** were baptized, and there were added that day about three thousand souls.

Holy Spirit thrilled life.

Titus 2:9 Bondservants (Stewards) are to be submissive to their own masters in everything; they are to be well-pleasing, not argumentative, not pilfering, but showing all good faith, so that in everything they may adorn the doctrine of God, our Savior. For the grace of God has appeared, bringing salvation for all people, **training us to renounce ungodliness and worldly passions, and to live self-controlled, upright, and godly lives** in the present age, waiting for our blessed hope, the appearing of the glory of our great God and Savior Jesus Christ, who gave himself for us to redeem us from all lawlessness and to purify for himself a people for his own possession who are zealous for good works.

GOD is love, and God is inside Believers and therefore Believers have the seed of all love inside us and Believers should display the fruit of the love inside us. When Believers move outside the GOD-centered actions to self-centered actions the Holy Spirit inside Believers is grieved. Listen to Paul and Jesus in these scriptures;

Ephesians 4:29.

Let no corrupt communication proceed out of your mouth, but that which is good to the use of edifying, that it may minister grace unto the hearers. And **grieve not the holy Spirit of God**, whereby ye are sealed unto the day of redemption. Let all bitterness, and wrath, and anger, and clamor, and evil speaking, be put away from you, with all malice: And be ye kind one to another, tenderhearted, forgiving one another, even as God for Christ's sake hath forgiven you.

Mark 3:5

And he said to them (Pharisees), "Is it lawful on the Sabbath to do good or to do harm, to save life or to kill?" But they (Pharisees) were silent. And he looked around at them with anger, **grieved at their hardness of heart,** and said to the man (with the withered hand), "Stretch out your hand." He stretched it out, and his hand was restored.

Luke 16:10

"One who is faithful in a very little is also faithful in much, and one who is dishonest in a very little is also dishonest in much. If then you have not been faithful in the unrighteous wealth, who will entrust to you the true riches? And if you have not been faithful in that which is another's, who will give you that which is your own? No servant can serve two masters, for either he will hate the one and love the other, or he will be devoted to the one and despise the other. **You cannot serve God and money."**

The question is always the same self-centered or GOD-centered" are you treating others as you would have them treat you? Are you feeling compassion to serve others in need? This continuing question is not leading Believers to be a missionary to Africa, but instead to bring every thought to the Lordship of Jesus Christ "to love others as God has loved you". Constantly concerned with others before yourself.

Remember, you are GOD's beloved, God wants you to be prosperous so that you can be a blessing, instead of needing a blessing.

Those purposing to be rich fall into temptation and lusts that plunge men into ruin and destruction. The great gain comes from **Godliness with contentment. Purposing to be a Steward of GOD's abundance and content with your destiny. Considering others more significantly than yourself.**

The Beginning.

Also by the Author

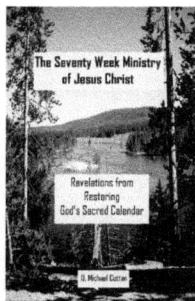

The Seventy Week Ministry of Jesus Christ:
Revelations from Restoring God's Sacred
Calendar
by Michael Cotten
ISBN: 978-0982480274
260 pages, $15.99

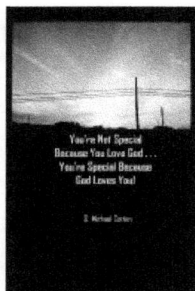

You're Not Special Because You Love God . . .
You're Special Because God Loves You!
by Michael Cotten
ISBN: 978-1936497034
110 pages, $14.99

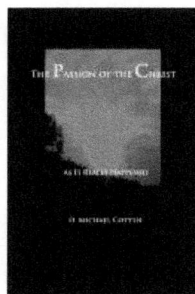

The Passtion of the Christ: As It Really
Happened
by Michael Cotten
ISBN: 978-1-936497-19-5
197 pages, $16.99

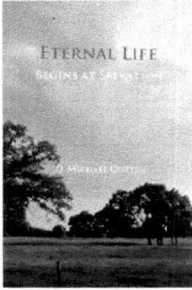

Eternal Life Begins at Salvation
by Michael Cotten
ISBN# 978-1-936497-25-6
101 pages, $14.99

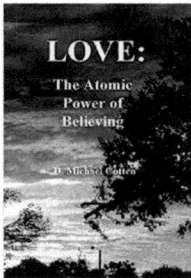

Love: the Atomic Power of God
by Michael Cotten
ISBN# 978-1-936497-33-1
115 pages, $14.99

Searchlight Press
Who are you looking for?
Publishers of thoughtful Christian books since 1994.
PO Box 554
Henderson, TX 75653-0554
214.662.5494
info@Searchlight-Press.com
www.Searchlight-Press.com

Where Is Your Holy Spirit? 154

www.ingramcontent.com/pod-product-compliance
Lightning Source LLC
Chambersburg PA
CBHW071754090426
42737CB00012B/1815